TRUMPE W9-CLQ-781

Uniform with this volume

FLUTE TECHNIQUE
by F. B. Chapman
Fourth edition

OBOE TECHNIQUE
by Evelyn Rothwell
Third edition

CLARINET TECHNIQUE
by Frederick Thurston
Third edition

HORN TECHNIQUE
by Gunther Schuller

TROMBONE TECHNIQUE
by Denis Wick
Second edition

RECORDER TECHNIQUE
by A. Rowland-Jones

In preparation

ORGAN TECHNIQUE
by Peter Hurford

HARPSICHORD TECHNIQUE
by Trevor Pinnock

Trumpet Technique

DELBERT A. DALE

Second edition

Music Department
OXFORD UNIVERSITY PRESS
Walton Street, Oxford OX2 6DP
1985

Oxford University Press, Walton Street, Oxford OX2 6DP
London New York Toronto
Delhi Bombay Calcutta Madras Karachi
Kuala Lumpur Singapore Hong Kong Tokyo
Nairobi Dar es Salaam Cape Town
Melbourne Auckland
and associated companies in
Beirut Berlin Ibadan Mexico City Nicosia

Oxford is a trade mark of Oxford University Press

First published 1965
Second edition 1985

ISBN 0 19 322128 4

Printed in Great Britain by
J. W. Arrowsmith Ltd, Bristol

Note to the Second Edition

I continue to be grateful to Mr William Overton (recently deceased) formerly principal trumpeter of the BBC Symphony Orchestra and Professor of Trumpet at the Royal Academy in London, who (in 1964) read my original typescripts and provided valuable criticism and advice.

I am indebted also to Mr Philip Jones. Mr Jones began his 35-year trumpet playing career at the Royal Opera House, Covent Garden, and has played principal trumpet with all the major orchestras of London. The Philip Jones Brass Ensemble has performed on numerous tours around the world including two tours of the U.S. He is also currently editing a series of brass music publications for the Chester Music Company. I appreciate Mr. Jones' reading of the present revision and his collaboration in the section on orchestral excerpts. His comments are most valued.

Thanks go also to my good friend Mr Charles Gorham who formerly taught at the Baldwin-Wallace College and performed with the Cleveland Symphony Orchestra. He is at present the Chairman of the Brass Department at the Indiana University School of Music, and is one of the founders of the International Trumpet Guild.

PREFACE 1

Sources concerned with the basics of trumpet performance are relatively numerous. However, Delbert Dale's presentation is concise, deliberate, and definitely helpful to the performer, both young and old, as well as to the trumpet teacher and particularly the general instrument music teacher. Mr Dale sets forth his topics and information in a clear manner. His verbal descriptions and suggestions are mainly traditional in scope and offer the serious teacher and player a source for continued development.

Bloomington, Indiana   Charles Gorham
March 1, 1983

PREFACE 2

Anyone wishing to know the 'ins and outs' of learning to master the trumpet will find this book (revised and updated from its first edition) an invaluable addition to their library. Mr Dale's down to earth non-dogmatic approach to both teaching and playing is apparent throughout. That he constantly emphasizes the development of technique, in all its guises, to musical ends is, I think, of the greatest value to the serious trumpet student. And, while pointing out that there can be no short cut to a proper command of the instrument, he offers, in each chapter, practical advice on how to gain the necessary skills to become a fine trumpet player.

London, October 1982   Philip Jones

CONTENTS

FOREWORD

There are at present several fine trumpet study and method books of all grade levels on the market, easily available to the trumpet student. Such books will help the student throughout his entire learning career. The college student, moreover, may refer to hundreds of theses (through inter-library loan) devoted to particular aspects of the trumpet; works on the history and construction of the instrument, its use in ensembles and in the band and orchestra, others on technical aspects of playing, on the repertoire, etc.

It is, though, somewhat more difficult to find a simple handbook of trumpet playing which will touch, however lightly, on most or all of these topics. It has been my purpose here to provide such a book, though emphasis has been placed on those technical aspects which are of immediate and practical use to the average student. It was my aim to present a short (and economical) textbook of some of the technical problems one may meet in the study of the trumpet and to suggest some solutions to those problems. The chapters on embouchure, breathing, tone, etc., should be of particular benefit to beginning and intermediate students. And with the addition of such chapters as those on the use of the trumpet in the orchestra and on repertoire, I have tried to make it useful even to advanced students of the trumpet.

I have purposely left out the subject of transposition, though it is indeed a very important aspect of the trumpet player's technique. Transposition is mainly a problem for the orchestral player; others are only seldom confronted with having to transpose their parts from their instrument's original reading key. Though some teachers like to start transposition study fairly early in their student's training, it is of little practical value. The jazz trumpeter sometimes finds it necessary to play something in a new and strange key to him, but this too is a case of being able to hear in any key (relative pitch) and has little to do with the actual mechanics of transposition. In the chapter entitled 'The Trumpet in the Orchestra', it is my thesis that the orchestral trumpeter is concerned with not one, but several differently-pitched trumpets. Thus to present a detailed explanation of all the transpositions would require many explanatory examples, too many for the limits of this short book. Besides, I contend that transposition is really not technically difficult for most students, though it may seem so at first. It only requires many hours of reading experience. It is not that the student must learn to read in a foreign language; it is more like having to read just one language IN CAPITAL LETTERS, or *in italicized ones*.

Most theories presented here should be of basic use to most students of the trumpet, but I can only suggest that they make their own comparisons and experiments. I encourage all students to search continually for as many solutions to their problems as possible, for only through a great amount of investigation and analysis can each player finally settle on the right solution for himself.

I

THE INSTRUMENT AND THE MOUTHPIECE

A glance at the history of the modern trumpet should, I feel, be beneficial to the aspiring trumpet student. By looking back, he may grasp a new insight into the structural problems of the instrument, how those particular problems affect and influence the player's technique, and lastly how he may adjust to, and overcome, such defects as are inherent to the trumpet.

For all practical purposes, we may begin at that point in the history of the trumpet when it finally became a musical instrument (in contra-distinction to those variously named trumpets used prior to this time mainly as mere signalling devices by armies and at various ceremonial rites), and when the possibilities were being explored of using the trumpet in concert performance. This took place some time during the Renaissance; that is, between A.D. 1400 and 1600. Prior to that time the prototypes of the trumpet were very simple instruments capable of sounding only a few pitches. Obviously, for a musical performance, something better was needed.

It was gradually discovered that by lengthening the instrument and using a proper mouthpiece, the higher partials of the overtone series natural to all cup-mouthpiece instruments could be produced. Thus, by the time of the Baroque era (seventeenth and eighteenth centuries), the trumpet had evolved into an instrument some seven or eight feet in length, wound around on itself. By playing within the range from the 4th partial up to about the 16th partial (a few very outstanding players could evidently reach even higher notes), it could be used very effectively (see Ex.1). Indeed, as the trumpet is still usually defined as an instrument possessing a bore which is mainly cylindrical in shape, the Baroque trumpet was, and remains, the most aristocratic member of the whole family of trumpet: approximately four-fifths of the length of this trumpet was completely cylindrical. As we shall see in the following chapter, the splendid brilliance and radiant tone of these long trumpets cannot, unfortunately, be duplicated on our modern shorter ones.

Ex. 1
Harmonic series of Baroque trumpet in C (8 ft. long)

Of course, the Baroque trumpet also had serious drawbacks; several of the partials were quite out-of-tune, and since it was a valveless instrument and effective only in the upper partials, the task of the trumpet player was certainly a difficult one. This, plus the fact that composers were constantly seeking new uses for the trumpet which demanded a greater flexibility, led to refinements in construction. They were (1) the invention of a slide-trumpet (German, 'zugtrompete'), which had a substantial vogue in Germany and later in England, (2) a trumpet that could change keys by inserting different-sized crooks; and, later (3) the invention of the valve trumpet. Those in the first two categories had obvious faults due to their unwieldiness and their popularity was relatively short-lived. Around the beginning of the nineteenth century, however, several almost simultaneous inventions pertaining to the valve led to an instrument quite similar to that which we use today. Within the next hundred years several trumpets, pitched in various keys, had short periods of popularity, but gradually the Bb trumpet (approximately 4½ ft. in length) became the most generally used. And though in recent years the C trumpet (slightly smaller yet than the Bb) has somewhat replaced the Bb in many of the world's largest symphony orchestras, the Bb remains the preferred instrument in most orchestras and bands. In brass bands and in jazz bands and studio orchestras, too, the Bb is exclusively used.

To interested students seeking additional information on the history of the trumpet, I recommend them to look into the history of the 'cornett' (a wooden instrument with keys and tone holes much like our present day woodwind instruments, but played with a cup mouthpiece), the 'keyed trumpet' of Anton Weidinger (for whom Haydn and Hummel wrote their fine concertos), and the whole family of bugles which evolved into the modern instruments of the brass band.

Notes on the construction and tonal qualities of the trumpet and cornet

The prevalence (or absence) of upper partials in a given sound distinguishes one tone colour from another. That is why we discern a difference between the sound of a piccolo and a flute, or the difference between the french horn and trombone, or for that matter, the variation between the piccolo and the trombone. The chief characteristic of most brass (cup mouthpiece) instruments is that there is an enormous wealth of these upper partials. The construction of the instrument has of course a large bearing on this tone factor, and by making slight changes in the design of the instrument, it is possible not only to change the tonal timbre, but also to vary the response of these upper harmonics in playing them as notes. Thus, an instrument with a large bore, somewhat conical in shape and played with a deep cup mouthpiece, will possess a warmer and darker tone than one which has a narrow and mainly cylindrical bore and is played with a shallow mouthpiece. This is the outstanding difference (besides the addition of the valves) between the modern short trumpet and its ancestor, the long Baroque trumpet. Herein lies also the difference between the trumpet and the cornet, for the latter has an even more conical bore than the modern trumpet, and is usually played with a deeper cup mouthpiece. The fluegelhorn is still more conical, and has a larger bore than the cornet, hence an even darker sound.

Both the modern trumpet and the cornet, however, have similar defects due to the similarity of design and because they share a common fundamental (B♭). It is impossible to build a three-valve instrument so that all the approximately thirty notes in the normal playing range will be perfectly in tune with each other. For instance, the 7th partial is so badly out of tune that we never play that note. High B♭ is never played open—but played 1st valve (the 8th partial using that valve combination). The 5th partial on each valve combination is also quite naturally flat (see Example 2). Thus most present-day trumpets fall into the following pitch-pattern:

Ex. 2
Modern Bb trumpet harmonic series (written C sounds concert Bb)

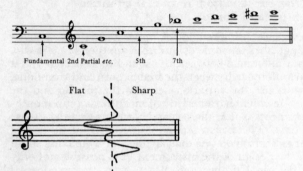

Dotted line represents true intonation

Moreover, though the separate valve slides are fairly well in tune when played singly, when they are used in combination they become gradually sharper as more and more tubing is used. Thus, the valve combination 1-2-3 is sharper at every point on the scale than when any of the three is played by itself. For this reason, most piston valve trumpets come equipped with a third valve slide finger ring and a thumb key or ring on the first valve slide in order to help correct these deficiencies. Added to this is the fact that with only one bell and one mouthpiece to serve seven differently pitched valve combinations (in effect, seven different sized trumpets), the tone varies as more and more tubing is used. This is because of the different relationship between the bore and the total amount of tubing, or length, of the instrument.

Selection of a good trumpet or cornet

All of the above should be taken into consideration in

purchasing an instrument. First in importance, I believe, is the matter of intonation. The student must choose an instrument that is as much in tune as possible when *he* plays upon it. Obviously, everyone has a distinct method of producing a tone on the trumpet. One will play with a tense and somewhat pinched embouchure. He will normally have to pull his main tuning slide out farther than the player who uses a looser lip formation. Adding tubing to the natural length of the instrument (or pulling out slides) seriously affects the intonation and response of the instrument, so that the tuning should be checked against the player's normal playing pitch. If the instrument's main tuning slide must be pulled out quite far to agree with this pitch, then that particular trumpet should not be chosen. Moreover, some slide must be left (to push in), in order to raise the pitch when the occasion demands. Trumpets are built with recommendations from good trumpet players who use good embouchures and good air systems, so that if, for example, a good quality trumpet is being played out of tune by the student, it is probably a case of the student using a poor embouchure or poor air support.

Next in importance is the general response of the instrument. Does it seem fairly easy to get a note to speak without having to 'blast'? Does the resultant tone have a vibrancy to it, neither too shrill and brilliant nor too dull and colourless? The mouthpiece has a great influence on these factors of tone, intonation, and response of the instrument. Often the student will blame the instrument for defects which are in fact caused by a poor mouthpiece.

It should also be noted that the demands placed on a trumpet by a professional player are not those required or even desired by an amateur or beginning student. Most players, even advanced ones, and certainly all those of lesser abilities, must not purchase a 'large' bore trumpet, for this would be just as bad as buying the proverbial 'pea-shooter' or small-bore trumpet. Even many physically mature players cannot cope with an over-large horn. Thus, a medium bore, or at most, a medium-large bore, should be selected for the beginner.

In purchasing a used instrument, be sure that the valves are in good condition. If they can be wiggled sideways in the valve casings then they are too loose and will leak, and considerable efficiency of the instrument will be lost. Also, be sure that the metal has not worn thin through too much use, or by several overhaul and relacquer jobs. Many professionals never have an instrument overhauled and relacquered or replated. The acid soak and buffing required to replate or relacquer a trumpet seldom leaves it in as good playing condition as it was originally.

Many teachers recommend that all beginners start on the cornet. Because of its slightly different bore relationship and design, it has more resistance built into the instrument which makes it somewhat easier to blow and gives it a little more flexibility than the trumpet. Besides, the beginner will have more of an opportunity to participate in band playing to which this instrument is better suited. This author would advise any young student to start on the cornet, if for no other reason than that it is simpler to hold and that this will in turn aid the young player in developing a good posture while playing.

However, the student should obviously seek the best professional advice available in choosing a proper instrument.

Care of the instrument

The instrument should be flushed out once a week with luke-warm water. Some say that soapy water should be used, but I feel that this is unnecessary if plain water is used regularly. First fill the instrument with water, depressing the valves, and then blow it out. Do this several times. Then, taking out all the valve slides, simply hold them under a tap for a few minutes each. There are small brushes available which may be run through the main tuning slide and through the mouthpipe. After doing this, the valves must be taken out, wiped with a soft cloth (also carefully run a soft cloth through the valve casings), and re-oiled. The slides must be wiped and greased again with a very thin coating of Vaseline or slide grease. Be sure not to let any excess get into the open tubing. The valves should be oiled daily with a special valve oil obtainable from any dealer. The third valve slide and first valve slide must move effortlessly since these will often be used on the out-of-tune notes. If this cleaning procedure is done weekly, then no other effort need be made.

The mouthpiece

I shall address my remarks in this chapter specifically to the orchestral trumpeter, or to the student who intends to pursue this type of work. The jazz player or lead player in one of the modern jazz bands very often depends upon a somewhat unorthodox mouthpiece to be able to meet his special requirements. Especially in the larger bands, he is chiefly concerned with finding a mouthpiece with which he may last through long and tiring performances and one which will make his high register easier. Unfortunately, this is often done at the expense of good tone quality. If such a player were to use a large mouthpiece, i.e. one with an extremely wide or deep cup and with a large throat or bore, he would find it practically impossible to endure the long hours of his work. He must of necessity choose a smaller mouthpiece.

The symphonic trumpeter is mainly concerned with a mouthpiece that will afford him a large volume of tone, more flexibility, and which will allow him to play both fortissimo and pianissimo in all registers over a shorter duration of playing time. He is also very concerned with sureness of attack and response.

Before going on to the selection of a proper mouthpiece, we must first examine the various parts of a mouthpiece and find out how each influences its overall capabilities. It must be noted that all the various parts are interrelated, and one separate part is important only in its relation to the rest of the mouthpiece (see Fig. 1).

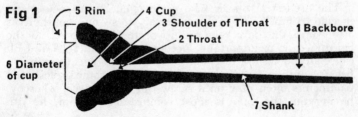

Fig 1   5 Rim   4 Cup   3 Shoulder of Throat   2 Throat   1 Backbore   6 Diameter of cup   7 Shank

Throat and backbore

This lower section of the mouthpiece has much to do with both the intonation of the mouthpiece and to its resistance. If the resistance is increased or decreased, naturally there will also be a marked difference in the flexibility and endurance of the player. The backbore, or that part of the mouthpiece which extends from the throat to the lower end of the shank, can flare out rapidly or it can be of a more straight or cylindrical nature. Usually only this factor of the mouthpiece is different between the cornet and trumpet mouthpiece; the cup and rim are generally the same for mouthpieces of both instruments. If the backbore expands rapidly (that is, a larger bore), the tone will naturally be larger in volume. This, however, will decrease the resistance of the mouthpiece, having the effect of 'pulling' the player's lips into the mouthpiece, and his endurance will suffer comparatively. A small backbore will have the opposite tendencies. The resistance will be increased, thereby allowing the player better endurance, but the tone will be smaller.

The backbore should ideally fit the bore of the mouthpipe of the instrument. The end of the mouthpiece shank should meet fairly well with the end of the mouthpipe of the instrument. When the difference here is too great, a considerable efficiency of the mouthpiece and instrument is lost.

The throat of the mouthpiece is generally cylindrical in shape. The length of the straight portion of the throat has a large effect on the intonation of the mouthpiece and instrument generally. It is necessary to keep the throat and backbore of the mouthpiece clean by occasionally running a small brush through it. Many careless students do not take care of their mouthpiece and one often sees a mouthpiece whose shank is dented.

The orchestral player who quite often has to peform on piccolo trumpets will find it necessary to switch mouthpieces also, since the bore relationship of the mouthpiece to the instrument is so important. Piccolo trumpets in F, G and B♭ especially need to be played with a smaller mouthpiece because of their extremely small bore. Thus, some professional trumpeters often play on a screw-rim mouthpiece, whereby, having the rim that is most comfortable to him, he can immediately change to different sized cups and backbores as the different instruments demand.

Cup diameter

The diameter of the cup decides just how much of the lips will vibrate, thereby directly affecting the tone and flexibility. A large cup diameter will allow a larger portion of the lips to vibrate inside the mouthpiece and will thus result in a larger volume of tone. Vincent Bach, one of the world's leading mouthpiece manufacturers, recommends the use of 'as large a cup diameter as the player can endure to play upon', and this is indeed very sound advice. Almost all symphonic players use large mouthpieces in order to obtain the rich tone and increased flexibility needed in their work. The large cup diameter tends to open the lips a little more. However, the student whose embouchure is not yet so well developed should be careful not to use a mouthpiece whose diameter and volume is so large as to encourage such a habit. Nevertheless, a large cup diameter will permit more freedom of lip movement in the mouthpiece and therefore it should feel more comfortable on the lips than a mouthpiece so small as actually to cramp their movements.

At first, the student switching to a larger cup diameter mouthpiece will find the higher notes a little more difficult to produce. With a reasonable effort, working on endurance, on lip slurs and long notes, he will discover that he can soon regain control of the higher register. Although a smaller mouthpiece to some extent encourages the use of mouthpiece pressure against the lips, the student will find that this added pressure for high notes will be of little help with a large mouthpiece, and he will soon learn to negotiate the higher notes correctly through proper embouchure development.

Cup volume and shape—shoulder of throat

If one could cut several trumpet mouthpieces in half, the variety of shapes which can produce a standard volume would be seen to be almost endless, although there are limits to the overall volume capacity of the trumpet mouthpiece cup. There are V-shaped cups, bowl-shaped cups, ones with a sharp or rounded shoulder, double-cups etc.

Generally speaking, the larger the volume of the cup, the more full and dark the tone. This is particularly true if the shoulder of the throat is open. Thus, a V-shaped cup will have a mellower tone quality, and though some cornet soloists prefer this deeper cup in order to emphasize the characteristic cornet tone quality, it is not very satisfactory when used on the trumpet, where a more brilliant tone is usually desired. Most symphonic trumpeters, and especially studio musicians, will use a more bowl-shaped cup in order to get the brilliant sound necessary for their work.

A shallower cup will brighten the tone and response and attacks will be easier, and if the point where the shoulder meets the throat is sharp and not too rounded or flaring, the attacks will be easier. Fig. 2A has a quite sharp curve going into the throat, whereas Fig. 2B has practically no shoulder at all.

Fig 2

A   B

Bite

The 'bite' or inner edge of the rim, or the point where the rim meets the cup, also is important because of its influence on the precision of attack. A sharp edge here will greatly assist the precision of attacks and response of the tone. A mouthpiece that does not have a sufficiently sharp edge at this point will not allow the lips to vibrate freely; and this should be particularly kept in mind in selecting a mouthpiece for the piccolo trumpet. Preferably this 'bite' should be set low in the cup so as not to cut the lips.

Rim curvature and diameter

This is the part of the mouthpiece which comes in direct contact with the lips, so comfort is the all-important factor to consider here. Nevertheless certain factors must be kept in mind, since even though a mouthpiece might feel very comfortable on the lips at first touch, it may prove, after only several minutes of playing, to be disastrous to the embouchure. For example, though a wide cushion-rim mouthpiece may at first seem particularly comfortable, it is a fact that such a rim will tend to clamp down the lip muscles, depriving the player of flexibility. Since the mouthpiece rim is large and spread over a larger area of the lip, the excess pressure is not too noticeable at first, and the player will thus tend naturally to use this added pressure to make up for his lost flexibility. Only too late does he realize that he has indeed used too much pressure. The use of a narrower rim mouthpiece will give the player more flexibility, but one that is too narrow may hurt the lips. Thus for more players, a medium wide rim is the best compromise between the cutting effect of the narrow rim and the bad habits that accrue from using one that is too wide.

Specially made or custom-built mouthpieces

There are now hundreds of different sized mouthpieces on the market, readily available to the student. For this reason, specially made mouthpieces need not normally be considered. To begin with, the extra cost of such a mouthpiece does not ensure that it will be any better than a regular stock model, and if the mouthpiece is damaged or lost, it might not be readily replaceable. Some manufacturers of trumpet mouthpieces can supply their stock mouthpieces with screw rims. This is a good purchase for players who may wish to change mouthpiece cups when switching to the piccolo trumpet, etc.

Selection of the mouthpiece

Even taking into consideration what has been discussed in this section regarding the trumpet mouthpiece, it is not an easy thing to select the ideal mouthpiece which is best suited to each player's embouchure and to the style of playing he wishes to develop.

The beginning student is basically interested in obtaining

results as quickly as possible, even though his embouchure is not yet fully developed and his lip muscles are weak. But just because these lip muscles are weak and delicate, it is extremely important to find at the very beginning a mouthpiece that is as suitable as possible. Preference should definitely be given to a good medium-sized mouthpiece—one that will be small enough to assist normal development of the high register in the early weeks, but large enough to allow the student's embouchure to develop normally and to produce a good tone.

Do not expect to find the 'perfect' mouthpiece that will do everything, alleviate all the problems. The mastery of the trumpet, it hardly need be said, depends mostly on the talent and industriousness of the student and the equipment he uses is only of secondary importance. Do not choose a mouthpiece just because some friend or famous trumpeter uses it and seems to get good results. The selection of a mouthpiece must be a personal choice. If the beginning student has adequate advice to begin with and selects a proper-sized mouthpiece, he will have little reason to change mouthpieces for several years, or until the time his embouchure is fully developed and he can physically cope with a larger and more professional model mouthpiece. Changing mouthpieces constantly is a very bad habit. By using one mouthpiece over an extended period of time, the student can train the same set of muscles consistently and constantly; witness the accuracy of the professional trumpeter, who in all probability, has used the same mouthpiece for ten or twenty years or more.

The advanced student who has already developed his embouchure will wish for a larger mouthpiece. With it he can acquire the larger tone and greater flexibility and sureness of attack demanded of the professional player. Finally, the main consideration in the selection of any mouthpiece should be tone quality. Ease of playing should be of secondary importance to tone.

II
EMBOUCHURE

It need hardly be mentioned that, to wind players of all sorts, embouchure is of absolute primary importance. This is especially true for the trumpet student. The woodwind player has several keys on his instrument with which to progress from one register to another, or even one tone quality or intonation to another. But the trumpeter, with only three pitch changing mechanisms at his disposal, must rely upon his embouchure not only to negotiate notes in the different registers, but also to give him basic control over tone, flexibility, intonation, attacks, etc. Thus the trumpet player's embouchure, in some measure, takes on duties that the woodwind player may give in some part to the tone holes and keys and to the reed of his instrument. For, as I have stated previously, the trumpeter's two lips do indeed represent, in the matter of producing a vibrating air column, the double reed of the woodwind instruments, or the string of the string instrument.

Practically all the trumpet student's technical progress will depend directly upon the efficiency of his embouchure. It has been my experience that students with a good embouchure can, through diligent study, surmount all other technical problems. There are, however, some students who seem never to be able to grasp how the embouchure must be formed to operate effectively. Some of these are students who have what appears to be quite normal physical qualifications for the trumpet, but were never taught correctly by a competent trumpet teacher, and have thus developed so many bad embouchure habits that breaking them is almost an impossibility. Others have something less than ideal dento-facial factors and are unsuited to playing the trumpet. It is the author's opinion that 5 out of 10 children should not be started on the trumpet, even if their desire is only to play in the school band.

Many bad embouchure habits emanate from the fact that virtually all beginning trumpet students start playing in the extreme low register—usually from low C to second line G. There are some valid reasons for this: (1) almost all students can easily produce these notes with their natural lip position, without setting an embouchure, and (2) if started in a band or ensemble class, they can almost immediately start playing with the other instruments in the class. Unfortunately too much time is spent in this low register learning rhythms, reading, etc., and by the time the playing register is extended to some of the higher notes, the student has already developed a manner of playing that never considered the upper register at all and will not work there. Many of these students do not develop their upper register to the point of playing successfully the range necessary even in a good school band, let alone what is required of the professional player.

Other instrumentalists in the band or orchestra do not experience the problems of developing the entire range of their instruments nearly as much as the trumpet student does. On all string, percussion and keyboard instruments, embouchure problems of course do not even apply and the extension of their playing register is automatic. The reed instruments basically only change their embouchures whenever they employ the register or octave key once or twice to cover the entire range of their instruments. But on the trumpet, where the overtones are only four or five notes apart in the low register (i.e. C and G are both played open), and even less in the upper register, the embouchure must markedly change and in reality must flex with every note in order to produce a good sound and good intonation. Therefore, a student of the trumpet, no matter what his age or degree of ability, must constantly be concerned with the development of his embouchure, if he expects any measure of success. It is here that we must begin our study of trumpet technique.

Dento-facial factors

Most people have minor dento-facial irregularities of some sort; over- or under-sized lower jaw, teeth which are crowded, protruding or spaced far apart, teeth which are extremely large or small, long or short lips which are extremely thick or thin, or which sport a 'lobe' in the centre, and lip textures that are unusually weak and flabby. Of course, many students have fairly normal relationships of jaw, teeth and lips. They should generally experience few difficulties with their trumpet embouchure if they have a really competent trumpet teacher early enough. But large irregularities of any sort will often interfere with correct embouchure adjustment. So I suggest that the student analyse his own physical structure to begin with, for it is quite possible that a problem in embouchure adjustment may be caused by some little deficiency here. Those who do find some such irregularities in their physical make-up should not be disappointed, however, since many such minor deficiencies can be remedied, providing only the student is aware of them and accordingly works to overcome them.

Ideally the trumpet student should have at least four strong and even front teeth, and as these are the base of the mouthpiece, the more square and flat they are, the better. Slight spacing of the teeth evidently has little effect on the embouchure, but of course extreme spacing of the front teeth might cause some problems. I have had several teachers and parents question me concerning the tooth structure of particular students, who are seemingly less concerned about the formation of the lips and jaw. But I am much more concerned with the formation of the lips (particularly the upper) and the jaw position, which in my experience, are far more important considerations.

Discrepancies in the form or size of the lower jaw will affect the positioning of the teeth and lips, which in turn serve as the support of the mouthpiece. Most people have a slight retrusion of the lower jaw; only a few have malocclusion, or protrusion of the lower jaw. When either of these are exaggerated, the student can expect most of his embouchure difficulties to originate from this. However, retrusion or protrusion if not exaggerated, can usually be corrected by learning to 'position' the lower jaw. And although this may at first seem awkward, the student can in time make it habitual to the point where it seems the natural thing to do.

Finally, let me say that though dento-facial characteristics must certainly be considered in starting the beginner, it is a fact that many students with seemingly extreme physical disadvantages, can adapt themselves remarkably well, providing they are aware of their problems and have the perseverance and industriousness to surmount them.

Lower jaw position

As has been alluded to earlier, the incorrect placement of the lower jaw is one of the most prevalent problems amongst trumpet students. Fig. 3A below shows a player with a retruded lower jaw, and as the foundation (lips and teeth) of the mouthpiece is slanted, it is natural for this player to play with his instrument pointed downward. Fig. 3B shows a base which is perpendicular, and then, naturally, the instrument will point more directly out.

Fig 3

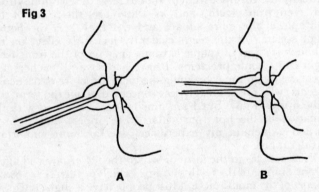

A   B

With the spine, neck and head erect, most professional trumpeters seem to hold their instruments at about an 80° angle out. A player such as Fig. 3A will: (1) have poor contact between his lips, (2) his upper lip will usually overlap his lower lip to some extent—sometimes quite extensively, (3) will have virtually no control over the direction of the air stream, and (4) will tend to let his lips enter the mouthpiece, especially in fortissimo playing. The inner edge of the mouthpiece is, or should be, fairly sharp, and this sharp inner edge will then cut the lip and the player's attack and endurance will suffer. A player such as Fig. 3B will allow his lips to lie more on the flat surface of the rim and his lips will not tend so much to enter the mouthpiece. Since his lips are not overlapping, he will have much better control over his air stream, with correspondingly better range, tone, flexibility, endurance, etc. Thus A must try to thrust out his lower jaw so that his teeth are more directly in line with each other, if he is to enjoy the advantages of B.

One must also prevent air pockets in the lower and upper lip and in the cheeks, and keep the chin flat. Some students (usually those with a severely retruded jaw) also tend to hold their jaws too far apart. This results in too much of the lips being unsupported in the centre and the airstream destroys the set of the embouchure when it passes through the lips.

I would advise the trumpet student to develop an embouchure which has a symmetrical appearance to it, as much as possible. Examples A, B, and C below are not symmetrical.

Fig 4

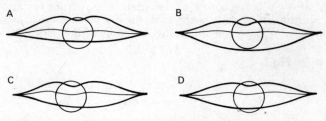

Example A shows an embouchure which has either (1) more 'roll' in the lower lip than in the upper (the height of the red part of the upper lip is greater than that of the lower), or (2) the upper lip is overlapping the lower to some degree. If that is the case, the air can only be blown at a downward angle. Example B is just the opposite of A, with correspondingly contrary results. Example C is of course totally asymmetrical, since the mouthpiece is off-centre, the right side looking totally different from the left side. While few professional players play exactly dead-centre and may be found to place the mouthpiece a little off to one side, it is also true that students whose embouchures are markedly off-centre rarely succeed to a professional level. Example D is the ideal. The height of the upper lip approximates that of the lower and the right side equals the left. A player with this embouchure, besides having more control over the airstream, has balanced use of his facial muscles.

Function of lips and lip muscles

The important factor here is not so much the size or thickness of the lips, but the texture and the muscular flexibility of the lips and the formation of them. Lip flexibility can be somewhat tested by having the beginning student 'buzz' on the mouthpiece, or by having him play simple lip slurs on the instrument.

The upper lip does most of the vibrating, and tension on this lip will govern the speed of the vibration. The shorter and faster the vibrating area moves, the higher will be the resultant pitch. An infinitesimal portion of the lower part of the upper lip must enter the course of the airstream in order to cause it to vibrate, and this portion of the upper lip must be its controllable part, not the fleshy or reddish inner side.

Fig 5

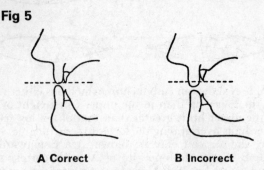

A Correct   B Incorrect

Thus, with the upper lip slightly rolled in, the lower edge of this lip should be more or less on the same line as the lower edge of the upper teeth (see Fig. 5 above). If this upper lip hangs too far down past the edge of the upper teeth, having no support there, the impact of the air stream can drive it into the mouthpiece, resulting in tonal distortion, poor endurance, poor attacks, and a lack of upper register.

The labial frenum which connects the upper lip to the gums extends to the inner lower part of the upper lip, and the muscular tissue surrounding this causes many upper lips to sag or protrude slightly right in the centre of the lip. This 'lobe' is a constant source of trouble, because the greater concentration of muscles and fleshy tissue is placed in the exact spot where the embouchure's aperture must be formed:

Fig 6

This 'lobe' must not be allowed to interfere with the air-stream, or protrude over the opening between the lips. By slightly rolling in this section of the lip, the upper lip can be held against the teeth in a straight line. Try this experiment. 'Buzz' your lips while watching them in a mirror, so that you can both see and feel the exact point where the air is striking the upper lip. If that point is on the outer dull-reddish part of the lip, then your lip is sufficiently rolled in. If that point is on the inner fleshy part of the lip, then it probably needs to be rolled in slightly more. The tendency for this centre section of the upper lip to slip out is greater in the low register and even more in fortissimo or tongued passages when percussive puffs of air slap against the tip of the lip. For the same reason, the tongue must not be allowed to come in direct contact with the lips in the normal tonguing action.

Allowing for muscular tension and relaxation then, the upper lip should remain more or less stationary *vis-à-vis* the teeth. Especially it should not rise and lower much when the pitch ascends or descends. The lower lip is responsible for adjusting the size of the aperture, or opening between the lips. Thus, the lower lip should tighten slightly in ascending, thereby increasing the tension on the upper lip; and it should relax in descending, taking the pressure off the upper lip and creating a larger aperture. For balanced tension, the lower lip should ideally be directly opposite, that is, perpendicular to the upper lip, moving directly up or down as the case may be. But even though the muscles of the lower lip are tightened or drawn up to create tension on the upper lip, it is not necessary to move the chin in the process. Keep the chin down and flat.

As far as I have been able to observe, players have two basically different types of lip texture, and there seems to be a definite relationship between this and embouchure adjustment. First, there are players with lips of a tougher and more fibrous nature (generally thin-lipped persons) whose lips do not tend to enter the mouthpiece but are firm enough to stay close to the teeth, withstanding the air pressure, and secondly, players with softer, fleshier lips whose lips do definitely have a tendency to enter the mouthpiece when playing. Those in the first category generally have fewer embouchure problems.

The centre of the lips: the aperture

The centre of the lips is where most of the attention should focus in any study of the embouchure. In teaching my pupils muscle focusing, I compare the aperture between the lips to the hub of a wheel with all the facial and lip muscles representing the spokes pointing towards the hub. Any muscle pulling or tension in an opposite direction from the centre will simply lessen the effort that should be directed to the centre. Actually, the centre of the lips should be somewhat 'puckered', but with the lips held firmly against the teeth and not allowed to protrude.

Though the lips do vibrate both by themselves and against each other at the sides of the aperture, they should not touch in the centre itself. This opening should be quite similar to the open end of an oboe or bassoon reed. In fact, we may say that the aperture used in producing the high register is similar to that of an oboe reed, whereas the one used for the lower register is like that of a bassoon reed. Thus the shape of the opening is similar in both registers, but enlarged or decreased by muscular relaxation or tension. In order to retain this standard opening on all notes, one must remember not simply to pinch the lips together in order to get the high notes. This results in a thin tone in the upper register (if it is acquired at all), poor intonation, and leads to the use of unnecessary pressure.

In moving from one register to another in intervals or scale passages, there is also an accompanying change in the direction of the airstream entering the mouthpiece, and of course, some action in the centre of the lips must make this possible. It is generally agreed, I believe, that the higher notes are produced by the airstream hitting close to the inside lower edge of the rim of the mouthpiece, whereas the lower notes will be produced by blowing straight into the mouthpiece. This can be tested by placing the hand directly in front of the mouth, in the way of the airstream, and then 'buzzing' the lips, gradually tightening the lip muscles and raising the pitch of the buzz and then descending by relaxing the lip tension. The direction of the airstream, it will be found, will indeed change, and the same sort of action of the centre lip muscles should take place when using the mouthpiece and instrument.

I have often suggested in this chapter that the student 'buzz' his lips in experimenting with his embouchure. I believe this to be an extraordinary exercise for the study of embouchure, to 'loosen' up the lips in warm-ups, and to develop lip strength. But I must point out that this 'buzz embouchure' is not quite the same as the normal 'playing embouchure'. Try this experiment. Buzz a middle G (second line), and while continuing the buzz, bring the mouthpiece and instrument gradually up to your lips to their normal position. Be sure not to change the set of your embouchure formation. The pitch should rise and a middle C or E will probably result. Now buzz a middle C and do the same thing. An even higher note should result with the normal light pressure against the lips. We may conclude then that the normal playing aperture will be larger than that of the buzz aperture of the same pitch, due to the tension on the lips caused by simple mouthpiece pressure.

Everybody has the potential for building up a tremendous amount of air pressure in their lungs, and if there is any conflict between the embouchure and the air flow, you can almost be certain that the airstream will dominate. Just as a tornado will destroy anything in its path, especially the weakest points; just as a powerful water course will weaken and finally destroy the weakest point in the dyke, the airstream can destroy the embouchure. Therefore do not pinch your lips together in the centre, but set your embouchure so that you *allow* and *permit* the air to flow freely into the mouthpiece.

The position of the aperture inside the mouthpiece has a huge effect on the range, flexibility, tone, etc., and problems are caused by the aperture being too high in the mouthpiece. Experiment with the placing of this aperture in the cup of the mouthpiece.

The corners of the mouth

The corners of the mouth should remain in approximately their natural position, held firmly but not rigidly and anchored in a stationary position against the teeth, so that they will not stretch outward or pull in towards the centre. Still, though they are held firm, they must not be too tense or hard, for any excessive muscle effort will simply detract from the control needed in the centre of the lips. Experiment with the corners in different positions; failure in endurance can often be traced to not having the corners positioned correctly. Excess stretch in the corners will have the effect of thinning the texture of the lips and will result in a thin pinched tone and a lack of flexibility. And this so-called 'smile system' invariably leads to mouthpiece pressure. Vice versa, if the corners are allowed to move in towards the centre, this will tend to push the centre of the lips away from the teeth and into the mouthpiece, resulting in a distorted fuzzy tone.

There is a greater concentration of lip muscles at the corners of the mouth than in the centre of the lips. These muscles must be developed in order to acquire the upper register and endurance in playing. Also, since we wish the air to escape from the lips through the centre, muscle activity should be strongest at the corners and weakest in the centre, so that the air will naturally be blown out there.

Fig 7

It will generally be found that those students with undeveloped embouchures will get tired in the centre of the lips (from too much mouthpiece pressure and pinching), whereas most professional players, when they tire from long hours of playing, will tire at the corners of the mouth, because they are using their lip muscles correctly.

Placing the mouthpiece

Much attention must be given to the correct placement of the mouthpiece on the lips. It cannot simply be haphazardly set on the lips; rather the student must find the one ideal position that will produce the best results for him. The mouthpiece must not feel merely perched on the lips. There must be a sensation of a 'grip', so that it feels like a natural extension of the lip muscles.

As the lips are very flexible and pliable, their appearance outside the mouthpiece, and their actual position inside, may seem very different. Thus I suggest that, for practice purposes, the student occasionally use a cutaway rim, so that he may see how his lips are operating inside the mouthpiece. As to the vertical placement of the mouthpiece, we find that professional players vary slightly in the proportion of lower and upper lip in the mouthpiece. I am of the opinion that the lips should as nearly as possible cross the mouthpiece at the point of the widest diameter, and that the farther this lip line (or aperture) is removed from this point, the more difficult it will be to produce either the extreme high or low register, or to obtain a resonant tone. Certainly it seems logical that the largest volume of tone will be produced by an aperture extended over this largest diameter.

I have encountered a number of beginning students who attempt to put just a very little upper lip in the mouthpiece. I believe they do this because they discover they can use the mouthpiece rim to help hold their upper, vibrating, lip in place through pressure. These students are found to blow up into the mouthpiece to obtain their higher notes, and are often found jutting their lower jaw out radically, and maybe even pointing their trumpet up over a 90° angle. Some of these students can play quite high and have fair endurance too—but none end up with a satisfactory tone. They have poor attacks (because their lip is pinned down), poor flexibility and no control. They never succeed in this manner.

Horizontally, the mouthpiece should be placed in the middle of the lips, as the tension of the lip muscles will then be equally distributed. Occasionally though, overlapping or irregular tooth formation makes it necessary to play slightly off-centre. In cases of this sort, the student probably should not change his embouchure unless his teacher strongly recommends it. If he has good flexibility and control and a good tone, he should probably remain in his most natural position. A few students who start without lessons from a qualified teacher, begin to play off-centre, even though their teeth, lip and jaw factors are entirely normal. This is another matter. Many of these students can switch to the centre, with the help of a competent teacher, and almost immediately learn to play as well and usually much better than they could before.

By far the largest number of students who are playing off to the side do so because their upper lip has a 'lobe' right in the centre of the upper lip. Some students seem never to be able to control this lobe, it easily blows out, overlaps the lower lip, shuts up the aperture and the student then discovers that the only way to get air into the instrument is to play over to the side. These students rarely succeed in this manner. This is one of the two most serious embouchure problems found amongst trumpet students.

After finding the most suitable and comfortable position for the mouthpiece on the lips, the student must take care always to place it in the same position. By doing so, he can consistently develop the same set of muscles and will more quickly learn control. For the same reason, one must always use the same mouthpiece, and not be switching back and forth between various sizes and makes.

Concerning mouthpiece pressure

The only use of mouthpiece pressure on the lips should be to prevent air from escaping between the lips and the mouthpiece. There is no 'non-pressure' system of playing the trumpet, contrary to what some would have you believe. There is, however, a 'light-pressure' system, and this is what the student should attempt to develop. A slight pressure helps to focus all the air into the mouthpiece. This is all that is needed; more is too much. With a light pressure, the lip muscles can be contracted and relaxed freely, which is impossible if there is a great force of pressure clamping them down. The pressure must be distributed evenly over both lips.

Excess pressure can result from various causes. Three of the main causes are; (1) use of the 'smile' system, which thins the lip texture, making it inflexible and weak, (2) other embouchure difficulties where there is not sufficient control in the centre (i.e. too much tension in the corners, or the upper lip not being rolled in enough), and (3) the attempt of young students, whose embouchures are not set properly, to play in the high register when their lip formation is simply incapable of doing the job. One word of warning; the pressure habit, once started, is most difficult to break!

The lips must maintain a constant condition of mobility. Thus I strongly advise the student to play with a 'wet' embouchure. In the first place, there is really no such thing as a dry embouchure after the first few seconds of playing. A wet embouchure allows for more minute and rapid changes. A student accustomed to starting with a 'dry' embouchure may at first find this a little difficult, but within a few weeks he will discover it to be very much easier.

Intonation

Many factors enter into the problem of intonation; and generally this subject will be treated in a subsequent chapter. My intention here is merely to point out the relationship of embouchure to intonation. The embouchure, besides being a contrivance to make a note speak, must be continually engaged in making those notes sound the correct pitch. The trumpeter must have a very intimate knowledge of which notes on his own instrument are out of tune and must be favoured, and also to what extent his lips must function to pull those notes into correct pitch. A weak embouchure generally will result in the low register being flat because the lip muscles are not held firm. In an attempt to acquire sufficient lip tension to make the upper notes speak, the player with a badly formed embouchure often over-estimates the amount of tension needed and pinches his lips together, with the result that the high register is then too sharp.

Even though the 5th partials (4th line D, 4th space E and Eb) are slightly flat, I often hear students play these particular notes horribly out of tune simply because their lip position is bad. If the equipment you are using is good, then these notes can be pulled into proper pitch quite easily providing the embouchure is correctly formed. Usually in such a case it is a matter of the player not having his upper lip rolled in sufficently, or he may have the mouthpiece set too low on the lips. If the upper lip is blown out, and protrudes into the mouthpiece, then almost no amount of lip tension will bring these notes into proper tune without ruining the tone quality.

Bad endurance also can often be traced to the embouchure in its important function of keeping pitch. If the player's lip formation is fairly well developed and he plays with diaphragm support, has good control over all registers, etc., he may be simply playing on the sharp side of all the notes. By constantly pinching each note, the lips soon become weary. This player might try pushing his tuning slide in farther, relaxing his embouchure generally throughout the whole compass of the instrument, and intentionally try to play at the lower edge of the note by using a larger aperture. Players who are unfortunate in having to play with others whose intonation is not good will soon find their endurance reduced for the same reason. The lips are very busy indeed in simply trying to make the notes speak and to produce a good sound on the trumpet, and if they must also work overtime trying to warp every note into proper pitch, they will soon become fatigued.

Exercises for developing the embouchure

Any student who is seriously engaged in improving his embouchure should have two very valuable pieces of equipment and should use them frequently in his study; (1) a mirror, and (2) an embouchure visualizer or cutaway rim of a trumpet mouthpiece. These two articles can simplify greatly the study of embouchure, since by visual means the student can clear up questions about proper lip function.

It is almost axiomatic that those students who can 'buzz' their lips really well also develop exceptional embouchures. I tell my students to remember three things when they practise buzzing:

(1) Be sure that the 'buzz' (or vibration of the lips) is even. It must have a real 'buzzing' sound to it and not a raspy, flapping, uneven sound. It must be done by the upper lip. Of course, if it is an even vibration, it will have a distinct pitch to it.

(2) It must be high pitched. For the sake of developing a trumpet embouchure, it does absolutely no good to buzz in the trombone register. Thus it must be in the range of third space C upwards, the higher the better. I have had at least one student who could buzz a double C. And be sure to buzz without air pockets in the lips.

(3) The buzz should be fairly loud. The trumpet is 4½ feet long. Thus a little wisp of air coming out of the lips is not going to do a whole lot when it is applied to the trumpet. You must move air.

After you have developed some capacity to buzz your lips, then try buzzing scales and arpeggios and familar tunes. Practise scales and arpeggios chromatically, going as high as you can with them, and when you can buzz a tune at one pitch, try to do it an octave higher!

I would recommend that students include at least the following in their daily warm-ups:

(1) Easy attack exercises. For instance, play a chromatic scale from second line G to G on top of the staff . . . . . *ppp* . . . . . minim (half note), minim rest (half rest), minim (half note), minim rest (half rest), etc. The whole object here would be to see that you get an immediate response with as little air as possible. Set your embouchure so that these notes start extremely easily, without pressure and effort, and right on time.

(2) Lip slurs . . . . . two note lip slurs . . . . . three note lip slurs and rips . . . . . and extended lip slurs over a 1½ or 2 octave span. By using the same valve combination on a given lip slur, and playing the same exercise, with rests in between, with all seven valve combinations (open, 2, 1, 12,

23, 13, 123) you will gradually loosen up your embouchure and gain flexibility. In playing these lip slurs, be sure to make the lip do all the work and remember not to resort to pressure or force of any kind. Attempt to make the slurs as smooth and rhythmically as possible. All lip slurs should begin in the middle register. In order to increase the playing range, extend these lip slurs up as far as possible until the tone becomes a 'static' note or squeak and finally tapers off to nothing. The further these squeaks or static notes extend, the greater the normal dependable playing range will become.

(3) Long notes. Long notes played $<$ $>$ require accurate lip control if the crescendo and decrescendo are to be balanced and the tone does not change its character or colour. In progressing to a louder dynamic marking or a softer one, the lips should remain as stationary as possible, with the air pressure making most of the change in volume. These exercises should begin as softly as possible (but with a good clear attack) and taper off likewise. There must be no change in the intonation of the note in the crescendo and decrescendo.

Developing the upper register

During warm-ups, during your general technical study, during your work on your high register, I think that it is very important to keep the lips feeling healthy and refreshed all the time. You cannot play the trumpet well if your lips feel tired and exhausted. Thus always rest according to the effort made.

From the very beginning, the student should try to develop simultaneously both high and low registers, always in his exercises revolving around the notes in the middle register. If he does not do this, he may develop, quite unconsciously, a 'double-embouchure'. Such a student will often be found to have a fair amount of facility in the middle register, but must change his embouchure to play in the upper register, and cannot combine the two. The 'double-embouchure' quite often is the result of the student relaxing his lips too much for the low notes (the fleshy inner part of the lip rolls too far out) and then when progressing to the higher notes, he finds that it is impossible to pull the lips back in, and the tone shuts off. The player must resist the temptation to relax his lip muscles completely for the low notes.

The higher notes necessitate a faster lip vibration. To accomplish this, the aperture must be decreased in size and at the same time, the lip muscles surrounding the aperture must be contracted so that there is more 'snap' in them. My own lip-movement formula for effecting this change in the lips is (1) a slight rolling in of the upper lip, (2) pulling the upper lip backwards against the teeth—but not by mouthpiece pressure, and (3) a balanced tension of the muscles of both lips—especially in the corners—pressing against each other—but still retaining the reed-shaped aperture.

Along with these changes in the embouchure, there must be a corresponding movement of the tongue. In the matter of tone production, the inside of the mouth and the throat (the oral cavity) resemble the organ pipe; a large tone chamber for the lower notes and a smaller tone chamber for the higher notes. Thus, as one proceeds from the low register to the higher register, the tongue should be gradually raised in the mouth as shown in Fig. 8.

Fig 8

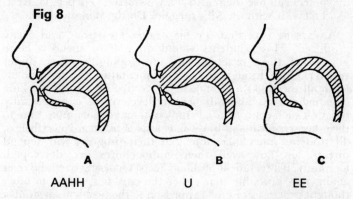

A	B	C
AAHH	U	EE

Exercises to develop the upper register should include the following:

(1) One note experiments. Start on a note which is fairly easy

near the top of your register, say a G on top of the staff. Just play one note. Rest. When your lip feels refreshed, play the next note a chromatic half step higher. Rest. Another half step higher, etc. You can do this type of exercise with your buzzing, or with the trumpet, finally going up so high your tone turns into squeaks. Keep going. Try this exercise played softly or loudly, but whatever way you decide to do it, try to make the next note you play as loud and as strong and as easy as the one preceding it.

(2) Lip slurs. Beginning at the top of the staff, on F♯ played 123, one can play scalewise with just one valve combination. Make up a three-note lip slur (F♯, G♯, A♯, G♯, etc.) and repeat two or three times. Rest. Do the same lip slur a half step higher (13). Rest and repeat up the valve combinations (123, 13, 23, 12, 1, 2, open). Be sure these exercises are done strictly with the lips and not with added mouthpiece pressure. This same exercise may later be done with four, or five, then six notes, etc. Also practise extended lip slurs throughout the entire overtone series.

(3) Singers use arpeggios and scales, sung chromatically, to develop their range, projection, and tone quality. Trumpeters can use them also. Play a slurred G arpeggio. Rest. Follow it with an A♭ arpeggio. Do the same with scales.

Always be sure that the high notes are strong and easily produced. Most students would do well to spend a large portion of their practice time developing an easy upper register. Only through much experimentation can the student learn all the tricks and knowledge needed for a good working embouchure. As his embouchure develops, he can gradually taper off such concentrated study of it and devote more time to the other technical and musical aspects of playing. Nevertheless, all students must take note that their progress will depend directly on how well their embouchures are developed. Certainly, if a technical problem keeps recurring over and over again, it is probable that either the cure lies simply in one's thought processes or one's approach to the problem, or, it may be something directly connected to some malfunction of the embouchure.

In conclusion

We have now discussed nearly all the factors pertaining to embouchure. In conclusion allow me to enumerate them here:

(1) The degree of 'roll' in upper and lower lip
(2) Degree of relaxation/tension in lips in the centre and at the corners
(3) Size and shape of aperture
(4) Position of lips on teeth
(5) Thickness or thinness of lips under the mouthpiece
(6) Position of the corners of the mouth
(7) Lower jaw position
(8) Spacing of front teeth
(9) Proportion of upper and lower lip in the mouthpiece (vertical placement)
(10) Horizontal placement of mouthpiece
(11) Placement of aperture in the cup of mouthpiece
(12) Amount and type of mouthpiece pressure
(13) Tilt of the trumpet
(14) Volume of air passing through the embouchure
(15) Speed of air passing through the embouchure
(16) Direction of air
(17) Tongue position (ah—u—ee).

For the benefit of students, I liken the trumpet embouchure to a 'recipe' for, say, a cake. There are literally thousands of different cake recipes, and each has numerable and specific ingredients that make up that particular recipe. Likewise a trumpet embouchure. Every player of the trumpet, whether good or bad, plays the trumpet in his own peculiar fashion, which consists of a mixture of the above factors. All these are 'recipes' for embouchure work, at least to some degree. In trying to improve some of the less efficient embouchures, if a student changes just one of the above ingredients of the 'recipe', chances are his playing will be immediately worse, not better. The same thing would happen to the cake recipe, if one would arbitrarily double or halve just one of the ingredients. When changing one of the ingredients, it almost always necessitates changing several parts of the mix. Thus, I would recommend to the student that if his teacher recommends a change, the student should not throw the idea out if he finds it results in a worse result immediately, but continue to experiment with it in conjunction with other factors until he can find a solution which will include the recommendation of the teacher.

III

TONE

Breathing

Before discussing the tone itself and its various qualities, we must first consider briefly the origin of the tone. By this I mean breathing and its application to trumpet playing.

I think that many teachers confuse their students with their explanation of the breathing process as it applies to wind instrument playing, and some go to strange lengths, with odd physical exercises, etc., designed to develop muscles and capabilities beyond those required for trumpet playing. It must be realized by the student that, after all, breathing is a natural and required process of life. To be sure, it is, in the average person, a quite unconscious function of his body, but its further development and application to trumpet playing, though there is a technique involved, is not unnatural or difficult to learn. In essence, it means simply bringing the breathing process out of the darkness of our unconscious and becoming aware of it and its uses through conscious thought. By intelligent and careful practice one can develop this breathing power to the extent where in performance it almost becomes habitual. I say almost, for it still must often remain a conscious effort, if it is to be used effectively and to its ultimate capability.

Let us first look at the possibilities in breathing and the various ways we all, at one time or another utilize our breath. For our purposes here, there are what I may term three fairly distinct kinds of breathing; (1) Diaphragmatic breathing, (2) Costal breathing, and (3) Clavicular breathing. Diaphragmatic breathing is that which we notice in the newborn infant—a slow rise and fall in the area around his stomach. There is a sympathetic co-ordination between the diaphragm (the thin partition which divides the chest cavity from that of the abdomen) and the intercostal muscles around the ribs. We observe costal breathing very often in a person who is preparing to lift a heavy object, as this type of breathing is a natural means of obtaining more air for purposes of unusual activity. The third type is clavicular, or upper chest breathing, which is noticeable in the physically exhausted adult who has just climbed a long flight of stairs and is gasping for air. I have pointed out the above types of breathing only in order to demonstrate that although the average person normally uses only about half his lung capacity in his regular activity, he does in special circumstances exercise the various parts of his lungs which usually lie dormant. The brass player must learn to use his total lung capacity and bring into action those parts of the breathing apparatus which the average person rarely uses.

To gain further insight into the breathing process, let us look at the physiological aspects of our breathing equipment. The lungs take up practically all the space of our chest cavity and are confined by the ribs and intercostal muscles on the sides and by the diaphragm (made up of muscles) at the bottom. The lungs and chest cavity are conveniently larger at the base than at the top, and we are aided in our breathing by the fact that the lower two ('floating') ribs are not fastened and are thus free to move. During a deep breath these ribs move outward, affording more room for the lungs to expand outwards, and at the same time the dome-shaped diaphragm membrane flattens out so that the lungs may expand downward. Immediately outside these organs lie the abdominal muscles. They too are superbly designed, for in the act of expiration of the breath these muscles serve to pull the ribs down slightly, thereby diminishing the air cavity, and at the same time to push up the diaphragm. All of this helps to produce an intense outgoing air stream. This short description is sufficient, I believe, for our purposes here.

Raphael Mendez, in his book *Prelude to Brass Playing*, gives a three-stage formula to remember in taking a healthy breath. It is very simple; 'Down . . . out . . . up!' I shall explain this more fully. By thinking 'down' and taking in our breath slowly and quietly, we should first feel a pressure around our waist-line. Then by continuing further with the same inhalation we should next notice the lower ribs expanding outward in all directions, in the front, sides, and even in the back. All that remains then to complete a full breath is to fill the upper portion of the lungs, at which time the chest will expand outward while the lower abdomen draws inward with a complementary action.

I hasten to add a couple of footnotes to this, however. Though I have mentioned a three-stage process, I must remind the student that this is a gradual process done with one uninterrupted flow of air, with no hesitation between the different stages. And it is to be remembered that in filling the upper portion of the lungs, one must not raise the shoulders.

Thus we have filled first the lower area of the lungs and then the upper portion. As a result the air is lying on that portion of our anatomy (the diaphragm and the abdominal muscles) which will quite naturally help us to expel the air. We have seen then that this air intake is completely natural, and the only 'abnormal' fact about it is that we have made a conscious effort to use all the facilities at our disposal and are free to control the output of air by learning to manipulate and use the diaphragm and abdominal muscles.

'Breath control', as regards wind instrument playing, simply means control of the expiration of the air. Here a detailed study must be made by the trumpet student, so that he may learn to use the air as effectively as possible.

During the emission of air, the gradual deflation of the upper chest or lung area will be followed by the gradual return of the abdominal muscles and diaphragm to their original position. This air must be pushed out of the lungs, through the chest, throat and mouth and into the mouthpiece in one uninterrupted flow with no disturbances caused by unnecessary muscle tightness in the same areas or organs. The airstream, with a small but continuous pressure behind it, should gently pass through the vibrating area of the lips (this point of contact should be felt) and not be impetuously blown into the instrument. I personally believe that any further control of the air stream in exhalation is more a matter of embouchure refinement, control of the tongue and larynx (both of which influence the size of the air cavity in the mouth), and purely musical considerations such as phrasing, volume, etc.

However, there remain some observations to be made of factors bordering on and adjuncts to the breathing procedure. It is hoped that the advanced student practises good posture while playing, but the beginning student must remember that it is virtually impossible to obtain a good breath and dispose of it correctly unless the body is erect, whether in a sitting or standing position. Air should most often be inhaled through the corners of the mouth. Particularly in taking a fast breath in a sustained passage this must be done so as not to upset or interfere with the placing of the mouthpiece on the lips. I suggest that the breath be taken in as inaudible a manner as possible (a quiet breath is usually more slow and deep). However, when time does not permit, the intake of air will quite often become audible.

The air should never be allowed to remain stationary in the lungs. For instance, there should be no hesitation between breathing in and blowing out. The only possible exception to this might be in setting for an attack on a note in the high register. And with regard to playing in the high register, it should be remembered that a fast expiration will aid the emission of those notes and will to some extent lighten the burden of the lips.

The type of mouthpiece used has much to do of course with the amount of air required. The resistance factor in trumpet mouthpieces varies a great deal and a large mouthpiece will require much more air than a smaller one. It might be well to note that this is just one more reason why the beginning and intermediate student should play a medium-sized mouthpiece until he has developed his breath and embouchure control to the point where he can successfully cope with a larger mouthpiece.

I have described above the procedure to be followed in taking a deep breath—a full breath. But although every breath should follow the same pattern (down, out, up), that is not to say that every breath taken for the purpose of playing the trumpet must be a full breath, for indeed that would be almost as bad as breathing too shallowly all the time. The length of the breath must be adapted to the length of the phrase to be played; the longer the phrase, the deeper the breath. Inhale only what is needed and no more. In short passages, long and frequent breaths must not be taken, for if some stationary air remains in the lungs for even a short while, a kind of panting will result because of incomplete exhalation. From the very beginning of the expiration of breath, the output of air must be controlled so that one is never short of air at the end of the phrase, and so that both end and beginning have all the firmness and volume needed. The student will find in his practice that different passages will require different degrees of control—some phrases have their high point (volume and intensity of tone) near the beginning where others might only come to their climax at the very end of the phrase or breath.

Another secret of good breathing is to breathe in time to the music. For instance, in a slow 4/4 time, if a phrase begins with a crotchet (quarter note) on the fourth beat of a bar, the breath should be taken on the third beat. Good timing in taking the breath initially, and proper breath control while playing, will open up many new possibilities for the industrious student. The modern trumpet player is faced with many long passages written by contemporary composers to be played in one breath, so he must develop his breathing capability to its fullest extent.

The only advice I may suggest in practising breathing and its application to performance is simply to think about it occasionally. On any technical exercise, test yourself to see how far you can go on and how many bars you can play in one breath. Then determine to go a bit farther the next time. Only by taxing your lungs and controlling apparatus can you develop this aspect of trumpet technique. The H. L. Clarke *Technical Studies* are excellent exercises for the development of breath control.

Vibrato

The use of vibrato and its obvious connection with the tone must be considered here. Vibrato is used to enhance and add warmth to the tone, and thus vibrato alone must not be considered as an end in itself. A vibrato that is too obvious to the listener is already exceeding the limits of good musical taste. And because of the naturally incisive quality of the trumpet tone, one must be very careful at all times to keep it under control. Vibrato should be used to help keep the tone alive and to give it vitality and character.

The student should spend most of his time working on his tone without using a vibrato. The use of vibrato should be limited to those exercises of a solo or legato nature where such a tone is desirable and of course omitted entirely on any rapid or unison passages and most tutti passages. Do not try to cover up any deficiencies in tone quality or intonation by using vibrato.

Vibrato, probably as much as any other aspect of technique, distinguishes one performer from another. Pop singers are probably more readily identifiable because of their individual vibrato than because of their style or tone quality. The same is true of other musicians. Concepts of vibrato vary with individuals as well as in the different branches of musical performance. Particularly there is a great difference between the type of vibrato used in jazz, pop and studio work and that of the symphonic player. The vibrato used in the jazz and popular fields is generally wider and faster than that generally used in the symphony orchestra. In classical music, it should be used sparingly. In most ensemble playing or in tutti passages in the orchestra, it is usually unnecessary and should be reserved for special solo passages only.

Even in solo legato passages, vibrato need not be used constantly. One of my favourite tricks is to add vibrato only after reaching a note and playing it straight for a short moment. See following example.

Ex. 3

Trumpet in C   Britten: *4 Interludes* (Peter Grimes)

Or, for instance, if a semibreve (whole note) at the end of a phrase has a diminuendo to *pp*, I sometimes start it with a vibrato and taper it off to a straight tone at the end until if fades out. Examples are the ending of the second movement of the Pilss Sonata and the ending of Enesco's *Legend*.

An uneven vibrato is useless and not in good musical taste: it must be of an even pulsation and width. I believe that most trumpet students would do well to develop a vibrato of between four and five vibrations per second. I have observed students producing vibrato by a variety of means, most of them incorrect. Some use a lip vibrato, some a hand vibrato, some by air in their throat, while others shake their heads or their instruments. The only two that should be considered are those made by the lip or by the hand gently rocking the instrument. Some very fine trumpet players have a beautiful vibrato made by the lip. Nevertheless, I personally discourage students from using a lip vibrato in the belief that the lips and the embouchure are already very busily engaged in starting the attack, producing the tone, in flexibility, and intonation, etc., and should not unnecessarily be taxed with the added burden of producing a vibrato.

Because of their lip vibrato, many excellent symphony players in the past would sound fine playing, say, Tchaikovsky or Sibelius, and not so good, for instance, on Gershwin. It has been my observation that most users of the lip vibrato usually have only one style of vibrato at their command, whereas those using a hand vibrato can easily change the frequency and amplitude of it. It seems that once you train your lip to quiver to produce a vibrato, it wants to move at that same rate no matter what music you are performing. This certainly should be of concern to those trumpet students who wish to develop an all-round capacity, to play symphony work (today's symphonic player must cope with a wider variety of musical styles than in the past) as well as popular, jazz, dixieland, etc.

I would accept most methods of gently rocking the instrument for the purpose of vibrato since they may be visually controlled and studied. I believe, however, that preference should be given to that method whereby the right hand gently moves to and fro along the side of the trumpet, parallel to it, and not sideways, or pushing against the instrument. We must mention that in this process, the hand, fingers, wrist and forearm should remain relaxed, not allowing any muscular tension or rigidity to interfere with the movement. Most of the movement can originate out at the elbow.

Some students may discover that using hand vibrato doesn't

seem to do the job. Students who are using a great deal of mouthpiece pressure normally will find that the extra slight pressure on the lips caused by hand vibrato simply has no effect on the tone. I would strongly advise such students not to adopt arbitrarily another type of vibrato, but to improve their embouchure to the degree where they do not have to use so much mouthpiece pressure.

Finally, in order to attain rhythmic perfection and to discover the possibilities of vibrato, I recommend that the student practise his vibrato with a metronome (a speed of 4 or 5 vibrations at M.M. 60, or 3 or 4 at M.M. 80) on long note studies. Certainly the student must cultivate a style, and not leave his vibrato (and therefore tone) development to pure chance. This is equally as important as any other technique on the trumpet.

Intonation

In preced. g chapters I have pointed out how both the embouchure and the mouthpiece affect the overall intonation of the instrument. Before going on to a more detailed explanation of the trumpet tone, I should like to discuss this a bit more. Intonation has such a tremendous effect on the actual sound of a given musical passage, that the average student (unless he is fortunate in having perfect pitch or really excellent relative pitch) should probably spend as much time training his ear and learning to apply it in his performance as he spends on the mechanics of tone production. For instance, in the following excerpt from Brahms' Academic Festival Overture, which is fraught with intonation problems, simple pitch factors assume probably an even greater importance than pure tonal factors.

The trumpeter must know the general relationship of each note in his part to the key or scale in which it is written. And in moving from one note to the next, he must be able to hear precisely the correct interval at which he must play the second in relation to the first.

Moreover, to the pitch of every note there is a 'low', 'centre', and 'high'; and generally speaking, the trumpeter must tune his instrument so that he will be able to play most of the notes

Ex. 4   Trumpets in C

on his instrument exactly in the centre of the pitch without having to lip any note too much one way or another. Let us quickly notice here that the player who finds it necessary to pull out his main tuning slide quite far to meet the proper pitch level, must probably also pull out his separate valve slides a little. I strongly advise against too much juggling of the tuning slides, since after the player has tuned (supposing he has done it correctly) the out-of-tune notes should usually be individually adjusted with the embouchure. However, in the symphony orchestra, and even when playing with fine musicians, the trumpeter may find that playing certain rare solo passages with the different sections might necessitate minute changes in the tuning.

Besides the purely musical problems of intonation, the trumpeter must always be concerned with intonation problems inherent in the trumpet itself. As we have found in an earlier chapter, to build a three-valve trumpet with a perfect scale is impossible. Referring once more to the chart on page 4, we find that trumpets are (1) flat on middle D, E♭ and E, and that (2) the low D and low C♯ are extremely sharp. In the case of the former, not much can be done except to lip them up, maybe with the help of the tongue (see chapter on embouchure). Alternate fingerings of the D by valves 1 and 3, E♭ for 2 and 3, E by 1 and 2, invariably sharpen these notes. Though in rare instances these alternate fingerings may be used, normally they should not, for the tone quality is quite inferior to other notes in this register. The low D and C♯ can be compensated for by throwing out the 3rd valve slide with the finger ring . . . . . approximately ½″ for the low D and about 1″ for the low C♯. Most trumpets are now provided with a 3rd valve slide finger ring attachment, and no self-respecting trumpeter can do without it. To acquire facility in its use is a whole technique in itself. See the following excerpt:

Ex. 5   Bizet, *Carmen* (trumpet in A)

Played on B♭ trumpet. Note alternate fingerings
X------extend 3rd valve slide ½"

X------extend 3rd valve slide 1"

Many professional model trumpets may now be purchased with a first valve trigger mechanism also. This mechanism is particularly useful on a C trumpet, for instance on the following notes: low E, middle A and E, and on high A. Many players have the tendency to pinch too much for the upper notes with the result that the higher register is somewhat sharp, and sometimes the use of the trigger may help here. These intonation problems directly connected to the instrument itself, unfortunate as they may be, must be constantly kept in mind.

Temperature affects the intonation, of course, and brass instruments can rapidly change pitch because of this factor. Brass band players who are occasionally required to perform outdoors must keep this in mind. And, in the symphony orchestra, where the trumpets are sometimes required to rest for several bars or even minutes, often the instrument will cool and the pitch will correspondingly drop. A few bars before beginning to play then, the player must blow air gently into the instrument, depressing all the valves, to warm it up again to the original tuning pitch.

I have observed student after student at contests who play out of tune (usually flat) for two reasons. Many students think they are warmed up when they are in fact not, and many never even get their instruments (particularly in the winter time) warmed up to room temperature, let alone up to breath temperature. Even if these students tune up properly at the outset, their instruments change in temperature so rapidly that half way through their selection they are playing at a distinctly different pitch level. Also, many amateur players tune at one level and perform at another, again, usually flatter. It seems that when these students tune up on only one sustained pitch, they tend to tense and pinch more for that one note, and then they play in a looser, more relaxed, manner in the normal course of their playing, with the result that even though they might have tuned perfectly in the beginning, their playing pitch level is substantially different.

Besides the study of actual ear training and harmony, I recommend playing as much ensemble work (duets, trios, quartets) as possible, for this is the best way to discover your own and your instrument's tonal peculiarities.

Tone

In beginning this section I must first make the confession that I truly wish I could draw upon a larger and more descriptive vocabulary—such as one might expect from a Sir Thomas Beecham or Leonard Bernstein—so that I could more forcefully impress upon my readers my concepts of the trumpet tone. I have concluded that herein lies one of the difficulties of teaching music students the techniques and concepts of developing a proper tone on their instruments. Much depends upon the student's ability to recognize and discern good intonation, good tone quality, balance, etc., so that he can improve these factors in his own performance. And the teacher's capacity to further the student's progress along these lines will depend upon his ability to use words and ideas and expressions to convey to the student an impression of this sound, or that nuance, or the proper timbre that is desired.

The student, particularly the young beginning student, is often so completely occupied with the technical aspects of simply playing the notes that he cannot, or does not, give much consideration in his early training period to proper tone production. I have already mentioned the means by which we may use our embouchure to improve our tone. If we look at this in reverse, we may see that by simply listening to the student's tone, we may discover whether his embouchure is correct or not. This is in fact the chief way to determine the effectiveness of his embouchure function and how to improve it. Thus the teacher must insist that the student devote much thought to tonal ideals and production even in the early weeks of his training.

Another serious impediment in teaching tone production is that of course no two persons have similar tonal ideals. Fortunately, however, the modern student has an opportunity to hear and to compare, either in live performances or through good recordings, the performances of outstanding soloists and orchestras and to choose what he likes and reject what he dislikes. This listening process must be encouraged to the fullest extent; careful and intelligent listening to other players in the concert hall and in rehearsals, and most important, in the individual's private practice room.

With the possible exception of the trombone and some percussion instruments, the trumpeter has at his command a tonal and dynamic range greater than probably any other orchestral instrument. And it is the student's responsibility, if he intends to become adept at his art, to develop every facet of this technique of tone. The trumpeter must learn to play at both extremes of the tonal range; from the strident and boisterous Wagnerian tone to the intimate and subdued sound of the small ensemble. In the symphony orchestra alone, two basically distinct qualities of tone are needed. First, the martial, fanfarish, and dynamic tone for certain brass passages (see Ex. 6A)), and secondly, the more mellow and flowing quality needed in the soft lyrical passages (see Ex. 6B).

Ex. 6A   Tchaikovsky, 4th Symphony (trumpet in F)

Ex. 6B   Respighi, *Pines of Rome*, offstage part (trumpet in C)

The trumpet player must learn precision of attack and tone, for the instrument itself is naturally of an incisive timbre and is very capable of obtruding itself even in tutti passages. I don't really believe that professional trumpeters are more mistake-prone than any of the other orchestral instrumentalists, but certainly if in the concert hall we hear a 'goof', we can rapidly identify it if it comes from the direction of the trumpet section.

The trumpet tone is produced by a combined action of the breath, tongue and embouchure. I have already discussed at length the role of the embouchure and the breath in tone production. The role of the tongue and the oral cavity is also of tremendous importance. Of course, the tongue is used to start the air flowing through the lips and into the instrument. In this function the tongue serves as a valve, an air valve. Though there are conflicting theories on exactly how the tongue should move in this capacity, we may at least say that the tonguing action is produced by the front or forward part of the tongue and involves some movement of the very tip of it. Whatever the exact movement is, the quicker it is performed the more precise the attack or initial start of the note will be. I call attention to this in this chapter because I believe that the actual sound of the attack (the moment the sound bursts out of the instrument) has a great deal to do with the sound of the remainder of the note—at least to the listener. In other words, the technique of attack and that of tone cannot and should not be thought of and studied separately. I mean this to include all notes, long or short. But in a rapid single-tongued passage, for example, where lengths of notes are very short, about the only thing that remains to the actual note being played (or heard) is the attack. If that attack is precise and clear, rhythmically correct, and exactly on pitch, the overall sound might well be pleasing, even if the player's real tone is indeed small.

In an earlier chapter I mentioned the importance of the position of the tongue in the mouth in connection with playing scales, lip slurs, etc. It also has an effect on the tone quality. The lower the tongue lies in the mouth, and the larger the air passage in the throat and mouth, the broader the tone should be. This leaves much room for the student to speculate and experiment in his practice. One other reminder; think of the tone as originating not in the throat or mouth, but from the depths of the lungs or the diaphragm area. Do not play from the throat!

Let me speak of 'projection' here for a moment. The vocalist studies it. The string player knows that if he doesn't keep his bow moving continually lightly on the strings, his tone will not carry far. I have heard trumpeters play with what might be termed a 'fat' sound when heard up close, but when heard several yards away the tone lost its bigness and sounded quite dull and colourless. On the other hand, I have heard other players with a seemingly small tone who are nevertheless capable of cutting through a 100-piece orchestra, chorus and organ and what-have-you, even when they themselves are not playing very loudly. What is this quality of tone which enables it to be heard in all its sparkling clarity at the back of an auditorium over a whole orchestra? I call it 'projection'. Certainly 'bigness' doesn't imply dullness; and 'smallness' does not always mean brilliance. I believe that its presence or absence in the tone, like the bowing technique of the string player, is caused by the amount of effort which the player finds necessary in order to produce the tone. In talking about the string player I used the words 'continually' and 'lightly'. Let us make the analogy this way. Continual movement of the bow on the string—constant breath support for the brass player; light bowing—general ease of playing. If these two factors are present in the trumpeter's performance, I believe that he will have all the projection he will ever need to be sufficiently heard.

We might consider here the distinct differences of a rifle and shotgun. A rifle is a gun which shoots just one bullet on a lone trajectory; a shotgun shoots a cartridge containing many small 'shot' with the result that when its cartridge explodes, the 'shot' are sprayed over a relatively larger area. Various trumpet tones take on much the same character. Some trumpet players play with a tone which has little body to it, but projects itself—like a rifle bullet—cutting through the ensemble to the point where it is offensive to the ear. Some 'lead' players in jazz bands intentionally use mouthpieces and medium-bore trumpets which will assist them, and they intentionally develop embouchures which will provide them with a condensed tone, one which has an 'edge' and a brilliance to it, so that they can project their tone over the rest of the ensemble. While this may be proper in this instance, that same tone quality would not do in the symphony orchestra or for the soloist. At the other end of the spectrum, many students with undeveloped embouchures virtually spray their air into the instrument—much like a shotgun cartridge exploding and fanning out—with the result that their tone is so diffused that it is dull and lifeless.

Contrast is also necessary in any musical performance. Let us note that volume markings are only relative guides to volume. A pp by itself has no meaning. It only assumes importance when compared to other volume markings. And often it will assume another meaning quite apart from that of mere volume of tone, of loudness of tone. Do not think of pp as meaning simply 'very soft'. Give it some character. It may mean subdued, veiled, diminutive, restrained, etc. ff may mean power, or heaviness, or vehemence, besides meaning 'very loud'. One must realize too that a Mozart f means something quite different from a Mahler f. You must think in descriptive terms if your performance is to be vibrant and colourful.

Study of tone

The study of tone on the trumpet should usually be done at between *pp* and *mf*, since the true quality of the tone can be more easily heard than when playing forte or fortissimo. Besides, a real pianissimo is more difficult for most students to produce with a pleasing tone quality than a fortissimo. In any study of tone on brass instruments, both lip slurs and especially long tone studies must be included. Such exercises, however, must be continued over an extended period of time if there is to be any real noticeable improvement. It accomplishes very little to decide to practise tone studies today and then forget it in favour of more interesting exercises for a month. Long notes can be practised at various volume levels and with a ⟨====⟩ or ⟨====⟩ . The most important thing to remember is to use as little pressure as possible and still maintain a steady solid sound. Such studies should begin in the middle register and continue from there in both directions. Avoid forcing the high register; go only as high as you can without excessive strain. Only very gradually can one work up to the high register. When playing these exercises the student must concentrate carefully on the exact quality of tone he desires and must take great care not to let any distortion hinder the tone.

One frequently observed cause of tonal distortion is simply the result of trying to play too loudly. If a student whose embouchure is not fully developed attempts to play too loudly, the tone will spread and consequently it will suffer a loss of resonance and intensity. Two other frequent distortions are (1) a shrill piercing quality in the upper register, and (2) a fuzzy and unclear tone in the lower register. In the first case the player must remember to try not to 'pinch' to get the high notes but to do it with correct embouchure, breath, and tongue action. In the latter case the lips must be more open and not touching in the centre if a clear, ringing tone is desired. Any forcing of tone or any sound that is produced by too great an exertion, even in the higher register, must be avoided. The trumpeter must learn to play easily and without excessive exertion and force, for such things will immediately show up in the tone.

Besides long note exercises, such studies as the operatic arias transcribed for trumpet in the J. B. Arban *Trumpet Method* (C. Fischer edition) are good exercises for the development of tone. Or, for that matter, any slow and lyrical song or melody can be put to the same use. Let me here caution the student that any written notation must not be taken too literally. With our system of notation, the composer is severely limited, since many things are impossible to notate precisely. But there is an advantage in this for the performer in that he is left to his own imagination and devices to play it in his own style and character, as long as it satisfies the bare outlines the composer dictated. The interpreter's manner of constructing a musically good representation of the composer's desires is all important.

In my own experience as a teacher and player, I have come more and more to realize the value of thinking out beforehand a concept of tone or style of playing, and then observing its eventual influence on performance. I can only urge the student to develop the ability to 'set' or think towards the proper mood, tone, and timbre and then transpose that thought or concept into terms of the instrument—discovering ways and techniques of putting the thought to practical musical use.

I am of the opinion that if a trumpet student has arrived at a point where he can definitely appreciate the quality of one tone over another, and he has established in his mind the type of tone quality he is striving for, he will eventually attain it. In other words, I think that if this tonal concept is well established in the mind, the physical apparatus will in due time provide the means to produce it. I also believe that tone is the one aspect of technique that, like wine, requires ageing and maturing in order to reach its full richness. I have had many outstanding school and college trumpet students who had near professional technique in terms of tonguing, agility, range, coordination, speed, etc., but I cannot ever recall hearing any trumpet student in their teens who had a really well developed sound. Thus I think that it is important first to establish a clean, easy sound on the trumpet as soon as possible. That can be done. Then, continually think and strive for a richer and more resonant sound, realizing that it may take some time to develop it.

IV

ASPECTS OF TRUMPET TECHNIQUE

When we think about technique as it applies to the instrumentalist, we soon discover that this subject is so broad and all-encompassing that we can only approach it through an examination of some of its components. In other sections of this book, the techniques of embouchure and of tone have been discussed. In this chapter I wish to cover some of the other aspects; particularly those which (1) are unique to the study of the trumpet, and (2) are constant pitfalls for almost all instrumentalists.

Lip slurs and lip trills

Perhaps a definition of a lip-slur would be helpful. It is simply any slurred combination of notes which must be performed on the trumpet without having recourse to the use of valves, thus obliging the embouchure to negotiate it unaided. As the trumpeter has only three valves (and seven possible valve combinations) to execute a three-octave range, such a lip-slur will often be met with. The practice of lip-slurs should most often be in their consecutive order: open (no valves), 2, 1, 12, 23, 13, 123. In working on lip-slurs from the middle register downwards, play in the above order. And in working from the middle register upwards (as in high-register practice), I usually have the student begin with the lower (123) combination, gradually progressing up by half-steps.

In fact, I think that most lip-slurs should start in the middle register, working both directions, even if the particular study being done is devoted to either extreme high or low register, in order that the student may develop one embouchure for the entire range of the trumpet. He must not set his embouchure for one particular register, and then have to resort to another completely different setting to play in the opposite register.

There is a great tendency to apply more mouthpiece pressure to the lips in order to reach the upper notes of a lip-slur, but this must be avoided. A lip slur must be done by the lips! Moreover, the tension and relaxation of the lips in moving up or down a lip slur should be basically an updown contraction of the lips, not a movement sideways with stretching at the corners of the mouth.

Those students who find they are having difficulty playing lip-slurs even in the middle register are usually those who are trying to play with their normal lip position, rather than with a set embouchure. The result is that when they attempt to contract their lips to play the higher note, they simply close off the aperture, the airstream loses its intensity or stops altogether and the note does not speak. Their only recourse then is to use mouthpiece pressure which shifts their lips into a new position, or to blow harder to force the note out. In either case, of course, the lip slur is no longer a lip slur and the extra force and effort will always be heard in the resultant sound.

On a two-note lip-slur in the middle register and upper register be sure to keep the air volume and speed constant. Blow air through the duration of each note: as much air at the end of the note as there is at the beginning, but no more.

A flexible tongue can also aid in executing a lip-slur over a wide interval, i.e. a four or five note lip-slur on consecutive notes of the overtone series, by enlarging or decreasing the air chamber inside the mouth. The actions of the embouchure and tongue must be well co-ordinated. Besides this, the extreme upper and lower register need the use of slightly more breath support. This must be considered on a lip-slur as noted in Ex. 7A below, if the tone and volume are to remain the same throughout. However, a two-note lip-slur, as mentioned above, does not require extra air pressure for the upper note (see Ex. 7B) as the two notes are so close together. In this case keep the airstream constant.

Ex. 7

I have known both professional teachers and players use the term 'lip-slur' and 'lip-trill' indiscriminately. Nevertheless, a trill is simply a rapid alternation of a given note and its upper neighbour. On the trumpet, most trills are done by the use of valves, but some are not, or need not be. I wish here to speak of the latter. In the middle and low register, where the intervals of the natural overtone series are large, the lip slur can only be done by properly executed lip movements themselves as described above. However, in the upper register, where the intervals of the overtone series become smaller, such as a two-note lip-slur (or lip trill) as that in Ex. 8, they can be more smoothly and rapidly executed by the use of a tongue movement.

Ex. 8

This movement is approximately the same as it would be in whistling the slur rapidly. For instance, by changing the position of the tongue rapidly (a sort of too-ee-oo-ee), one can, by setting the embouchure in a properly tensed position (favouring the upper note), play this trill entirely by the use of the back of the tongue. To be sure, in the symphonic repertoire it can only seldom be used. I have used it however, on the trills at the end of Ravel's *La Valse*, on the end of the second movement of Mahler's First Symphony, and on the Hummel Trumpet Concerto—playing on a B♭ trumpet in the key of E♭. The brass band soloist may use it more frequently in cadenzas etc.

Scales—fingering problems

For the ultimate in technique a student should memorize, in my opinion, a total of ninety-nine scales:

Major scales	12
Natural minor scales	12
Harmonic minor scales	12
Melodic minor scales	12
	48
Scales of 3rds on above	48
Whole-tone scales	2
Chromatic scale	1
Total	99

This should not be regarded as an overwhleming task by the student, if a little common sense is employed in thinking them out. At first, practise your scales slurred, and slowly enough so that you can hear perfect coordination. Faster speed will naturally result if coordination is good. In order to gain perfection in playing scales rapidly and cleanly, they often must be taken apart and practised to acquire a surer knowledge of fingering problems. For instance, the C scale may be practised as follows:

Ex. 9

Scales, moreover, practised slowly, are wonderful exercises for intonation and embouchure practice. The student must learn to flex his lips gradually in relation to the scale in order to ensure good intonation and a fluent sound.

Frequently one hears a rapid slurred scale passage that almost sounds like a smear or glissando because coordination of the embouchure, breath, and fingers is lacking. Everything must go up and down together. Scales should have a stair-stepped sound to them, and even on a slurred scale have a 'clicking' and crisp sound from one note to the next, not unlike that sound produced by a good clarinettist when he smacks his finger down over an open note hole. The fingers (with the tips on the valve caps) must be put down boldly and firmly, but without jarring the instrument. Try to get the same speed and finesse on the more difficult scales that you have on the easier ones.

Good finger coordination is 90 per cent mental and 10 per cent physical. Make your fingering exercises long exercises, as suggested in the Clarke book, so that reflexes may develop. For the study of scales and finger coordination, as well as breathing and breath control and range development, I highly recommend the Herbert L. Clarke *Technical Studies*, in my estimation, the best trumpet book on the market.

Articulation

Scales should be practised with various articulations and styles of attack. Emphasis should be placed on keeping each and every note the same weight, tone colour, volume and length. For instance, in such passages as Ex. 10 below, the last note of the slur must remain long so that it will have the same character as the first of the two slurred notes: the tendency is to 'chop' off the last note of a slur so that it in fact becomes a staccato note.

Ex. 10

Likewise students will often play the slurred notes slightly faster than the tongued notes, or two notes with easy valve changes are played out of rhythm with a following difficult valve change.

Attacks—tonguing

Producing good attacks is mainly a matter of preparation, simple preparation. Even players whose embouchures are quite well developed and are in most respects capable players miss attacks and 'crack' notes through simple carelessness. In soft legato passages which are mostly slurred, and when the tongue has been somewhat inactive over a period of several notes, an attack must often be preceded by a conscious preparatory thought. Such an attack requires usually a small additional effort concerning air. All attacks need proper breath support, so that when the attack is to be made, the air pressure will be sufficient to start the air column in the instrument vibrating again. Another preparation regards mouthpiece pressure: an excess of mouthpiece pressure 'freezes' the lips in a stationary position and thus makes it impossible to secure a good precise attack. Thus, if possible, take the mouthpiece away from the lips, even if only for a split second, or at least attempt to reduce the pressure before an attack, so that the embouchure may function properly.

Recognize that there are several kinds of attacks—soft, legato, hard attacks, sforzando, forte-piano, etc. In practising attacks, practise them usually softly, which requires a well set embouchure to start the note with the aid of very very little air and force. Sometimes go to the extent of practising soft attacks without using the tongue at all (as you would blow out a candle or match), and make the notes start exactly on time. Make up exercises employing various note lengths and volumes, with random selected notes in all registers to develop sureness of attack.

The actual role the tongue plays in making an attack is the source of contention among trumpet teachers. Some insist that the tip of the tongue strike the lower inside edge of the upper teeth; others say that it should hit higher up on the back of the teeth at the gum line or even on the roof of the mouth directly behind the upper teeth. Still others favour that method by which the tip of the tongue rests in the lower part of the mouth, lightly touching the lower teeth, the attack actually begun by the centre of the tongue (the forward centre) striking against the roof of the mouth, All teachers recommend, however, that (1) the tonguing action must be done with the front or forward part of the tongue, and that (2) the tongue should not move past the front teeth except in very rare instances, and (3) one should not move the lower jaw in the process of tonguing notes. I will not advocate any one of the above methods of tonguing at the expense of the other, for I find that I personally will in one instance use a certain method of tonguing, and in another, a different method. I cannot recommend a certain syllable likewise, for I know that I use them all ('tah'—'tee'—'tu'—'toh') in certain circumstances. I can only suggest the student experiments with all the different methods and chooses for himself which is the best. Of course more of the tongue will be activated in forte attacks than in pianissimo attacks, and a sforzando attack will require a more forced and decisive tongue action along with more air force.

The tongue must also operate correctly in its vertical movement. For an attack in the high register, the tongue must be more tense and arched, whereas for an attack in the low register, the tongue should be more flat and soft. Some teachers advocate a 'tah'—'tuh'—'tee' system of tongue positions in the various registers, low, middle, and high. Especially in playing a single-tongued scalewise passage, this vertical tongue action should be kept in mind; in ascending and descending the scale, the tongue gradually changes its position and texture in the mouth.

One other reminder in playing tongued notes is not to stop the tone with the tongue but by the breath; 'tu' 'tu' etc.—not 'tut' 'tut' 'tut'—the latter requiring two actions of the tongue instead of one. For the same reason, in practising rapid single tongueing, do not attempt to play staccato. Unfortunately, I believe, many trumpet study books (even the excellent Arban book) introduce the staccato note too early. For instance, at the metronomic marking of 120, playing semiquavers (sixteenth notes), one is producing single-tongued notes at the rate of eight notes per second! Only an extremely adept professional player can, at this speed, possibly demonstrate a difference between regular and staccato attacks. Since a really fine staccato attack is more difficult to produce correctly at fast speeds and with a good sound, I believe that the single-tongue study should first be practised thoroughly with a good firm tone quality. The staccato can wait until this is well developed. Tone, on any note, long or short, is still the most important consideration.

As the speed increases in rapid single tongueing, the length of the movement of the tongue must be decreased. Even with a shorter stroke of the tongue we must still produce a sharp attack on each note. The trick is to find out how to keep the tongue fairly relaxed in the mouth and still keep up a rapid pace, and good attack. As often as possible, practise with a metronome to ensure correct rhythm. Be sure to play always 'on top of the beat'.

Triple and double tonguing

I believe most trumpet teachers agree that the triple tongue should be studied before double tonguing. In the triple tongue ('tu' 'tu' 'ku') the K syllable is first thought of as a more or less bounced action of the tongue between two normally strong T syllables. But in the double tongue, the K syllable is found to be an equal partner with the T syllable, which is as it should be. Because of the unnaturalness of the K syllable, the study of the triple tongue must be started at a very, very slow tempo, the slower the better. Remember, there are no short cuts to this! An exercise such as that given below will permit the student to concentrate better on the new tongue movement and upon the resultant sound.

Ex. 11

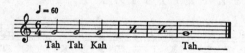

Tah   Tah   Kah   Tah____

For students just starting out on triple tonguing, I recommend the following four rules:

(1) Play loudly. (Most students only have good breath support when playing loudly)
(2) Hit each note hard. (You must make the K syllable a hard, abrupt attack)
(3) Play long notes—but
(4) Slightly separated

The tempo can be increased very gradually over a period of weeks. The problem is of course to develop the K syllable so that it sounds exactly like the T syllable, for the triple tongue as a whole must sound as nearly like single tonguing as possible. Thus, it is good practice to make up an exercise where you single tongue a series of notes—maybe four sets of triplets—and then triple tongue a similar set.

Practising just the K syllable by itself is also useful. The speed of triple or double tonguing must overlap the player's maximum single tongue speed. For instance, if the player can single tongue triplets up to m.m. 150, then he must develop a good strong and steady triple tongue at about m.m. 135 or 140. If the student can single tongue quadruplets up to m.m. 120, then he must have a good double tongue starting from about m.m. 100. This way, there will be no 'blind' spots in his technique.

Only after the student has developed his triple tongue fairly well should double tonguing be started. It should be practised in the same manner as triple tonguing; very slowly at first. The two following exercises are beneficial in strengthening the K syllable:

Ex. 12

Later the student must learn to mix up his single, triple, and double tonguing in any order without getting 'tongue-tied'. For example, the great majority of trumpeters must play the following excerpt from Sibelius's 2nd Symphony thus:

Ex. 13

My own tonguing procedure on the following from Stravinsky's L'Histoire du Soldat runs like this:

Ex. 14

Legato style—legato tongue

One would think that developing a sostenuto, or legato style of playing would be relatively easy to master. Nevertheless, it is in these easy passages that many players go amiss, by not following through with their air support and therefore producing a weak, sloppy sound. In legato passages it is very important to keep the air pressure at the embouchure as constant and unwavering as possible.

The trumpet tone is often described as 'brilliant', 'brassy', 'vibrant', etc., and often it is in one of these characterizations that the trumpet is used most resplendently by composers. There is, however, another side to this picture. Properly played, the trumpet is capable of setting softer and warmer moods. If many trumpeters have been slow to realize this potential in their instrument, composers have nevertheless been aware of the possibilities for quite some time. The second movement of the Haydn Trumpet Concerto, to cite just one early example, is written in a beautifully simple and warm legato style, but all too often we hear this and other similar passages played with the same hard attack that we might expect from a trumpeter playing a Tchaikovsky symphony. 'Cantabile' (in a singing style) is one of the most ignored musical markings by amateur musicians. It is as important to the trumpeter to learn legato-style playing and to develop a good dependable legato attack as it is for the string player to master the different styles of bowing.

At the outset of our study of the legato tongue, however, we are faced with a paradox. Tonguing definitely implies some sort of stopping of the tone (not, however with the tongue), in order to start the next one with a new tonguing action; and legato means a continuance or a sustaining of the notes in the melodic line. Obviously, then, an abrupt and accented attack would not be satisfactory in legato playing. Thus we replace the normally used 'tah' or 'tu' with a 'dah' or 'du' attack, which is softer and less accented and which is executed with a softer and more pliable tongue texture. As I have said, previously, in legato playing, it is most important to keep the air pressure constant and the airstream moving as much as possible to ensure a smooth style of playing. The tongue must move, in a legato attack, but it must not completely 'chop' off the airstream into separate blocks of air. I can usually demonstrate this more clearly to my students by simply telling them just to let the tongue 'dent' the outgoing airstream with a rapid flick of the tongue.

Intervals—arpeggios

The study of intervals and arpeggios is beneficial to the student in that they are ideal exercises for: (1) developing endurance, (2) developing a uniform tone quality in all registers, (3) improving intonation, (4) developing flexibility, (5) attack studies, (6) improving the range, (7) improving control. As an aid in developing endurance, I recommend the Arban book's interval studies, practised very slowly (m.m. 60) and playing each note as a minim (half-note), even though they are written as semiquavers (sixteenth notes). In that book, the interval studies last one line each. The student should play one line (in half notes), rest four or five seconds, and immediately proceed to the next line, etc. Practise this exercise pianissimo. Keep a daily record of how far you went with these exercises before the attacks and your control and your tone and endurance fall off—and the next day determine to go a few notes further.

Interval studies may also be used for intonation purposes—as always, careful listening and adjusting is required to make one note properly tuned to the one preceding it. Another important use for interval studies is to develop sure attacks and flexibility throughout the entire range of the instrument. An exercise such as the one below may be practised with varying volumes, with varying accents, and with various note lengths, i.e.

staccato, portato, tenuto. Later this same kind of exercise may be used to strengthen the double and triple tongue.

Ex. 15

Very important also is the use of such an exercise to develop slurring over wide intervals. A slur over a wide interval can be aided by the use of the tongue. For instance, at exactly the instant of making the slur with the embouchure and changing valve combinations, if 'du' or 'dee' is pronounced very, very softly with the tongue, the slur will sound much cleaner. Such a wide-interval slur must somehow skip over all the other notes in between, which are played with the same valve combinations, and it must not sound like a 'rip', hence the use of the tongue.

Ex. 16

Conclusion

Some time ago, reading an article on the technique of writing, I came across the following statement ' . . . writing is essentially thinking, or at least involves thinking as its first requisite' (Stephen Leacock, *How to Write*). I would like to apply that thought to learning trumpet technique. I believe that the actual development of technique is nothing more than a gradual process of developing good habits, and acquiring proper habits must be a slow and patient process requiring much thought. Many students, coming across a difficult passage, will fight and struggle with it, falsely believing that by simply going over it several times they will eventually correct the difficulty. But if the thought processes are wrong and bad habits are being employed, no amount of repetition will cure the problem. A little rest from blowing, and a great deal of patient thought, common sense and reason will cure many difficulties more rapidly than a thousand repetitions. Since the trumpeter must learn to play rapid, difficult and intricate passages fluently and effortlessly, any signs of struggle will simply be amplified by the trumpet and a musical performance will not result.

Technique is commonly thought of as speed pure and simple. And we often hear it said of some player who can play a fast scale or who can double- or triple-tongue rapidly: 'My, listen to that "technique".' But if that player, though he does have a fast tongue and rapid finger reflexes, cannot play an attractive, simple melody musically, he does not have technique. It is a fact that 99 per cent of our 'budding' young trumpeters will never be called upon to double-tongue the Flight of the Bumblebee in public performance. It is much more likely that in the normal course of his employment, the trumpeter will be required to play mostly minims, some crotchets, a few quavers, and only rarely a few semiquavers, with a great number of rests thrown in. The symphonic trumpeter receives his weekly pay because of his general musical ability, his sureness of attack, and his general reliability and dependability in hitting a few easy notes the same musical way every time.

V
PRACTISING

In the previous chapters, many of the main aspects of trumpet technique have been discussed. I wish to point out, however, that this short book does not purport to be a complete textbook. Even if I had expanded it considerably, added exercises, etc., I would still not consider it a 'do-it-yourself' study method. I know of only one programme that will provide the student with a good trumpet education, and that is: (1) frequent and regular lessons from a competent *trumpet* teacher —not just a music teacher who happens to know something about the trumpet, and (2) daily assiduous practice. Without these two things, continued over a period of several years, it is impossible to attain a real professional status.

Most students are quite incapable by themselves of adhering to a consistent and coherent learning schedule, and moreover, they are unable to recognize objectively their own weak points and correct them. This necessitates regular help and advice from a good teacher. But the daily practice session must be administered by the student himself. In this chapter, I will make a few suggestions which the student may follow in the practice session in order to achieve as much as possible in his daily studies.

First, the time and place. It is absolutely necessary to find a good, quiet practice room, free of outside disturbances. Avoid practising in an acoustically resonant room, since any echo or resonance will flatter the player's tone and consequently render faults less perceptible.

All force and excessive tiring are foreign to good study methods. It is a fact that, in comparison to other body muscles, those of the lips are small and delicate, and thus great care must be taken to keep them in a healthy and strong condition. Whereas the piano and violin student, using arm, hand and finger muscles, might be able to practise long hours each day, the trumpet student is limited to at best two or three hours of diligent exertion each day. Because of this necessarily limited time each day, the practice session must be carried out in a deliberate and sensible manner.

Beginners need only a few minutes a day to start. More time may be added as the lip muscles develop in strength. All practice should be done when the student feels fresh and alert (both physically and mentally) and thus morning practice is by far the best. Always attempt to keep the lip muscles feeling strong and robust.

To rest in proportion to the effort made seems to be a good maxim to follow. Of course some players will require more rest than others, but that does not necessarily mean that those players are less suited to the instrument. The student must learn his own endurance capability, and practise and rest accordingly. Moreover, it is mentally less fatiguing to rest and relax frequently. When the attack becomes less precise, or when the tone loses its usual resonance, or when flexibility starts to drop off, it is probably time to rest. Practise up to the point of tiring, but not much past that point. Two separate thirty-minute practice sessions are probably better than a one-hour practice session for the average.

Warm-ups

The first purpose of warm-ups is to help the player to become acquainted again with the feel of the mouthpiece on the lips. Just a few seconds of buzzing on the mouthpiece is the best method for some of getting reacquainted with it and to 'get the feel' of the proper lip setting again. Warm-ups, however, have other uses: (1) to build up lip strength (2) to increase flexibility (3) to increase the range (4) improve the response time on attacks (5) and immediately start thinking about tone quality, and (6) technical precision. The precise order of the warm-up routine varies with the player. Some like to do long tone studies followed by lip slurs; others, vice versa. Each individual must find the warm-up pattern which best fits his own needs.

Most initial warm-ups should be practised softly and easily, with practically no mouthpiece pressure. Herein lies one of the secrets of good practising. The student who practises softly and with little muscular effort most of the time, will obviously be able to extend his practice period a great deal longer than the one who gets a kick out of playing loudly and boisterously.

Some days the warm-up must naturally take a little longer, whereas at other times much less may be needed. But some form of warm-up should take place daily, even if time doesn't permit a complete practice session. I am of the opinion that many technical and musical problems emanate from the lack of proper warm-ups. School music students often have no time to warm-up properly, for instance before their ensemble practices at school, with the result that they are confronted with some heavy playing before their embouchures have warmed up to the task. The result is often tonal distortion, poor flexibility, poor attacks, sloppy technical precision, and a generally forced manner of playing that is contrary to a musical performance.

Technique

Again, what exactly should follow the warm-up period is a matter of personal choice, but any thorough practice period should, I believe, include three things: technique (used here in the broad sense of the word), some sight-reading practice, and a study of the repertoire. Technique practice can include (1) attacks, (2) lip slurs (3) tone (4) flexibility (5) scales (6) arpeggios (7) single tonguing (8) triple tonguing (9) double tonguing (10) legato studies (11) intervals (12) breath control studies (13) vibrato study (14) articulation (15) fingering (16) rhythmic studies and (17) register practice (high and low). I admit that to include a serious study of each of the above in every practice period would—at least for the beginning and intermediate student—be taxing in the extreme. Nevertheless, I suggest that, within practicable limits, the student make a daily and constant assault on all technical problems to keep from becoming 'rusty' or to prevent weak spots in his technique.

Sight-reading

Frequent practice at sight-reading is also important. The

professional musician spends a large part of his time sight-reading new music in the practice hall, in the recording studio, and occasionally, even in the concert hall. Recording artists frequently are sight-reading their music at the time of the recording session. And, the symphony trumpet player often finds himself not only sight-reading a new piece of music, but transposing it at the same time.

Repertoire

The study of repertoire should be done with distinct goals in mind. This, of course, is especially true in preparing for a recital or solo performance. Even without an immediate pending performance in mind, the student should daily attempt to expand his repertoire and performing ability, for it is here that he may put to practical musical use the time and effort he has spent on purely technical matters, and where he can realistically measure his musical progress. Once a solo piece has been memorized, keep it memorized. Don't forget it when you go on to the next piece. Go back frequently to these memorized pieces and see how they might be increasingly improved. The student, by sometimes practising previously learned material, can gain new insights into phrasing, musical interest and nuance, and technical assurance.

Let me digress here a moment to speak about metronomic markings for the sake of the uninitiated. They should not be taken too literally. It is a fact that a great number of the specified metronomic markings in many of the better étude books are all *but* impossible except for the most professional and virtuoso players. Sometimes these metronomic markings stand simply as a goal towards which to work. For the student, it is much more important to play your exercises in a technically precise and correct manner, even if the tempo is somewhat slower than desired. Only if this is done, can further speed and finesse result.

Whereas the metronome is a valuable tool in the study of purely technical matters, no solo work of any type need be practised or played from start to finish with mathematical precision, for indeed that would not lead to a musical performance. Such metronomic markings are only noted by the writer or composer to avoid gross errors of tempi.

Learning without the trumpet

I have mentioned previously the necessity of taking frequent rests from the actual playing time in order to rest the lip muscles, but these physical rest periods need not be wasteful in themselves, for there are many things the student can do to further both his technique and his general musicianship without actually blowing on the instrument. Does this sound ridiculous? Then let me ask how many advanced students of the trumpet are there among you who can whistle or sing through just a three or four line exercise correctly and come out exactly on pitch? There is much to be done in acquiring good pitch and intonation for purposes of trumpet playing, and much of this can and should be done in the rest periods. Industrious students need to learn harmony and theory and even keyboard, and this may be interspersed with your trumpet practising. Many embouchure problems may be studied best by studying the facial muscles and their movements in a mirror. Practise buzzing—always attempting to improve the quality, volume and range of the buzz. Practise buzzing scales and songs. Fingering problems can be conquered without recourse to blowing on the instrument. Rhythmic problems can be thought out previous to playing them on the instrument . . . . if you cannot think the proper rhythms, you are certainly not going to play them properly.

Single, double and triple tonguing must be practised first before trying it on the instrument. Again, always try to improve the quality of your 'tah-tah-kah', etc., by saying it and whispering it—and then later applying it to the trumpet. Be sure to keep your jaw steady—just like you must with the mouthpiece set on your lips—when practising tonguing. Practise your tonguing with a metronome.

Memorization can certainly be done quicker and better without the instrument. To become a musical performer, you must first be a critical listener. Take some time in your practice sessions to listen to recordings of good symphonic players and trumpet soloists. Listen critically to their tone, ease of performance, intonation, flexibility. Study the scores along with your listening. Students can record themselves on cassette or reel-to-reel tape recorders, and then play the recording back to study it. Spend some time this way in improving your technique and performing ability. All these things may be done in the frequent rest periods during the practice session without having to tire your embouchure unnecessarily.

Hints on study methods

The student should spend some time simply looking over the exercise he is about to practise, observing key signatures, possible rhythmic or technical problems, and making a mental note of dynamics, nuances, etc. This alone is a valuable time-saver. When playing, give particular attention to the quality of tone, intonation, and to style and phrasing, clarity of attack, etc. In general, avoid a vibrato style of playing, except in practising material of a solo or legato nature. Again, pianissimo practice is best as it is much easier to hear flaws in performance. It is needless and exhausting to play every exercise from start to finish. Work on individual sections and only put them together when they have been separately perfected.

The student

Allow me to make one personal observation very clear. Many, many more music students fail in their goals because of personality and character traits than ever fail beause of a lack of technical potential or even musical talent. Many students are not even honest with themselves. I have listened now to hundreds and hundreds of trumpet students, at the school level and at the college level, who would swear to you that they would 'do anything' to be a professional musician. And yet, they fail to understand and recognize the degree of motivation and dedication and perseverance needed to compete profession-ally. All of our physical actions, along with the quality of those actions, are initiated by the brain. Just as it is impossible to walk without 'thinking' walking, or sit without 'thinking' sitting, one cannot master any musical or technical problem without the correct thought pattern. A technical problem of flexibility, tonguing, fingering, attacks, tone production, etc. cannot be improved without the quality of thinking improving first. A musical phrase cannot be improved without first thinking better intonation, tonal colour, nuance, etc. Moreover, the improvement of our study habits, and the speed with which we are able to solve musical and technical problems are in direct proportion to the motivation and mental stimulus we possess.

'Nothing succeeds like success.' Attempt to achieve something new every day. The student must gradually learn to discriminate between good and bad playing habits and to analyse his own personal technical and musical problems. I wish to conclude this chapter by a quotation of Johann Altenburg, whose trumpet method, written in 1796, was one of the first such compiled. He said: 'If one only understands his art theoretically —that is, if he knows everything that pertains to it, but cannot perform on his instrument—he is no better off than the person who only knows how to criticize. On the other hand, if one is proficient on his instrument, but knows nothing about its theoretical basis, he is today numbered among the trade musicians. But whoever has learned his art theoretically as well as practically, of him it can be expected that he will continue to make great progress in it.'

VI

THE TRUMPET IN THE SYMPHONY ORCHESTRA

Paul Hindemith, in his book *A Composer's World*, expounds the theory that 'all music ought to be performed with the means of production that were in use when the composer gave it to his contemporaries.' He argues quite persuasively that most of the sounds emanating from our modern orchestral instruments are in fact 'counterfeit' to those the composer originally desired. The fact that the average modern-day listener evidently appreciates a heavier sound than that of audiences a couple of hundred years ago has led to an evolution in the manufacture of instruments. This is particularly true of the brass family of instruments, especially the trumpet. Indeed, though most of the orchestral instruments have changed somewhat in this period in appearance and in tone colour, still they were for the most part fairly well standardized by the time the symphony orchestra came into prominence. But the trumpet in use in Bach's time, for instance, was a completely different instrument than that which we use today. In approximately the last three hundred years the trumpet has undergone many basic structural changes, i.e. the addition of valves, and a shortening of the length of the instrument to about half that of the Baroque trumpet. And this three-hundred year period amounts to roughly the span of the normal orchestral repertoire.

In the first edition of this book, published in 1965, I commented that more could and should be done to manufacture more perfect replicas of old instruments, and that economically it was probably not feasible at that time to specialize on instruments such as the old Baroque trumpet and the cornetto.

I am happy to report that in the last fifteen years several interesting developments have occurred. First of all, modern day copies of such instruments are now more readily available, and they are substantially improved. Secondly, there is enough of a renaissance in the appreciation of such music, for one now to be able to purchase recordings of ensembles using natural trumpets, etc., and one can even hear in live performances groups specializing in this older music.

A number of excellent small brass groups have recently come into being that can now attract audiences around the world and a trumpet player sufficiently expert and interested in this type of performance can now make a living in this manner.

Another recent development of interest to trumpet students was the formation in 1976 in the U.S. of the International Trumpet Guild. This organization has a week-long annual convention of professional players, trumpet teachers and students, at which guest soloists and clinicians appear. For serious students of the trumpet, they sponsor two separate competitions, one a Concerto contest, and another, an orchestral audition competition. The Guild publishes one annual journal and three newsletters yearly devoted to articles on literature, special events, etc., and it also commissions new works for the trumpet.

For the trumpet player with sufficient capability, the symphony orchestra still however remains the most secure position, and the one that provides the most variety in terms of performance material. The principal trumpet player in the major symphony orchestras of the world must command the total range (up to high G above high C for the 2nd Brandenburg Concerto), a flawless technical capability, a musical concept that includes every kind of music from Baroque to rock, and the confidence and consistency of performance that virtually eliminates error. Most must rely on standard equipment to perform the myriad of tonal timbres desired by various composers and expected of the modern orchestral trumpeter. He must concern himself with the kind of equipment he must use to obtain the desired result.

He must acquire proficiency on three or four more differently pitched trumpets in order to perform well the basic orchestral repertoire. Sometimes he will even change instruments in the middle of a composition to facilitate certain passages. In switching to a piccolo trumpet, some will even use a smaller mouthpiece, in order to ease the high notes a little, and to get the lighter sound usually needed for piccolo trumpet parts. But

I would advise the student not to switch mouthpieces, except only in extreme cases. A few professional players can switch mouthpieces with little difficulty, but the average player will only end up cracking more notes.

Every professional examines his personal preferences, the fractional pitch and tonal discrepancies of his various instruments and how he may best alleviate the technical and musical problems of his part. Add to this the several different traditions prevailing in the major orchestras of the world and we find that trumpet playing is indeed a fine and complex art. For example, German and Austrian orchestras tend to use rotary valve and Bb trumpets more than American orchestras and generally tend to play with slightly heavier attacks. There are other European orchestras that prefer the C trumpet and particularly in France, the C trumpet is used almost to the exclusion of the Bb. Though it seems the 'French school' is currently undergoing some change to a darker sound, a few years ago one could always easily detect the French trumpet player because of his lighter, more brilliant tone. In Britain, trumpeters use the Bb principally and sometimes the C. In an American orchestra, the first trumpet players probably use a C trumpet about 80 per cent of the time.

To get a better picture of this, I have listed below some works out of the orchestral repertoire with prominent or solo passages for the trumpet and have noted my own personal preferences as to which trumpet to use, alongside those of Mr Philip Jones of the Philip Jones Brass Ensemble. This list then represents two different viewpoints of the use of differently pitched trumpets. Had this been enlarged to include other professional players' opinions, there would surely have been other ideas as to what trumpet is most effectively used in these particular works. These suggestions serve as a starting point for the advanced student who wishes to look into the possibilities of using various trumpets.

	Preferences	
	Mine	Mr Jones
BACH, J.S.		
Orchestral Suites No. 3 and 4	D	picc G
B Minor Mass	G	picc Bb
Christmas Oratorio	G	picc Bb
Brandenburg Concerto No. 2	picc Bb	picc Bb
BARTÓK		
Concerto for Orchestra	C	C (Eb from 211 to 255 in last movement)
BEETHOVEN		
Leonore No. 2 and 3—off stage calls	Bb	Eb and Bb
Symphonies No. 7 & 9	D	D
Other symphonies	C	Bb/C
BRAHMS		
Academic Festival Overture	C	C
Symphonies	C	C/D
BRITTEN		
4 Interludes from *Peter Grimes* (D part)	D	D
DEBUSSY		
La Mer	C	C
Iberia	C	C
Nocturnes	C	C
DVOŘÁK		
Symphonies 8 & 9	C	C
FRANCK, CÉSAR		
D Minor Symphony	C	C
HANDEL		
Messiah	D	D
Samson	D	D
Judas Maccabeus	D	D
Suite from *Royal Fireworks*	D	picc Bb/D
Suite from *Water Music*	D	D
HAYDN		
Most symphonies	C	C/D
Military Symphony (2nd trpt. solo)	Bb	Bb
Trumpet Concerto	Bb	Eb
KODALY		
Háry Janòs	C	C
LISZT		
Les Préludes	C	C

| | *Preferences* | |
	Mine	Mr Jones
MENDELSSOHN		
Symphonies	C	C
Midsummer Night's Dream		
(Wedding March)	C	C
Fingal's Cave Overture	C	D
MUSSORGSKY-RAVEL		
Pictures at an Exhibition		
—(muted part in Samuel		
Goldenberg & Schmuyle)	D	D
Remainder of above	C	C
PROKOFIEV		
Lt. Kijé (off stage part)	D	D
Remainder of above	C	C
The Love for Three Oranges	C	C
Symphony No. 5	C	C
RAVEL		
Piano Concerto	C	C
Daphnis and Chloé	C	C
La Valse	C	C
Alborada del Gracioso	C	C
RESPIGHI		
Pines of Rome		
(off-stage part)	C	C
Vetrate di Chiesa (solo in		
2nd impression)	D	D
RIMSKY-KORSAKOV		
Capriccio Espagnole	B♭	B♭
Suite 'Mlada'	B♭	B♭
Scheherazade	C	B♭
Le Coq d'or	C	B♭
SCHUMAN, WM.		
American Festival Overture	E♭	E♭
SCRIABIN		
Poem of ecstasy	C	C/D
SHOSTAKOVICH		
Piano Concerto No. 1	B♭	B♭
Symphonies	C	B♭/C
SIBELIUS		
Symphonies	C	B♭/C
SMETANA		
The Moldau	C	B♭

| | *Preferences* | |
	Mine	Mr Jones
STRAUSS, RICHARD		
Tone Poems (generally)	C	C
Thus Spake Zarathustra		
(octave jumps)	D	D
STRAVINSKY		
Firebird	D	C
Petrouchka (solo in Danse de		
la Ballerine)	B♭	B♭
(duet near end of		
ballet version)	D	D
L'Histoire du Soldat	B♭	B♭ cornet
TCHAIKOVSKY		
Capriccio Italien (8-bar		
solo passage)	E♭	B♭
Symphonies	C	B♭
WAGNER		
Parsifal Prelude	C	B♭
Tannhäuser March	B♭	B♭
Mastersingers Overture	C	C
WEBER		
Oberon Overture	D	D

The cornet also has its place in the symphony orchestra. Many composers call specifically for them in their scores, e.g. Berlioz, Tchaikovsky, Franck, etc. Most orchestral trumpeters perform these parts on the trumpet rather than taking the trouble to acclimatize themselves to another instrument. It is the author's opinion however that a composer such as Tchaikovsky, who had the genius to write the symphony to begin with, must have known the differences between the cornet and trumpet, preferred the use of the cornet in one instance, and the trumpet in another, and it behooves the artist player to follow instructions. Some conductors and a few of the more sophisticated orchestras now insist on using the proper instruments. The cornet can be used very effectively on some orchestral parts and in a great deal of chamber music because of the instrument's inherent flexibility. Such parts as in Stravinsky's *L'Histoire du Soldat* and the short solo in Tchaikovsky's *Capriccio Italien* lie particularly well for the cornet.

The intonation problems of the various trumpets generally become more acute as the instruments get smaller. Here too, there have been major improvements in the past several years. Manufacturers of top quality trumpets (in the U.S., particularly the Bach and Schilke companies) have made major improvements in the bell, the mouthpipe, and the bore of the C trumpet, D trumpet and smaller trumpets which alleviate some of the intonation problems. Still, on these smaller instruments, alternate fingerings must often be used on the out-of-tune notes (e.g. 4th space Eb and E).

Many composers seem to be unaware of the technical difficulties of the trumpet and they write in various transpositions quite carelessly. The Baroque and Classical composers may be excused, for at that time different circumstances prevailed. Modern composers, however, may not be excused, and it would, I believe, be a great aid to the trumpeter if all his parts were written, for instance, at concert pitch. Sibelius, for example, notated almost all of his parts for the F trumpet without regard to the actual key of the composition. And he did this after the trumpet had become a chromatic instrument and at a time when the F trumpet was only locally popular. I can see no logical reason for such a practice at all. At any rate, the orchestral trumpeter, besides being musically and technically proficient on his instrument, must be something of a wizard at transposition, and the wise student will begin tackling this problem also, as early as possible in his studies.

The cornet in the concert band

Having had the opportunity to experience both band and orchestral work, I have found that both fields of endeavour have their different musical rewards and their distinct musical and technical problems. If the trumpet is part of the 'dressing' in the orchestral score, the cornet, in the concert band is the 'main course'. In the orchestra, the trumpeter is asked somehow to blend and balance with instruments quite unlike his own, and at times he merely provides punctuation to a mainly string ensemble. The cornettist in the band, however, where the instruments are more closely related to one another, generally approaches his ensemble playing in a more homogeneous and subdued manner. Thus the approach to the whole problem of tonal balance and ensemble playing is slightly different; the trumpeter must attempt to take advantage of his distinctive sound, whereas the cornettist in the band must usually take refuge in his 'ensemble tone'.

A two-hour band concert can be exhausting in the extreme, and of course a heavy symphonic programme can be similarly tiring. Nevertheless it is different. We might make these comparisons to the tiring process of those of a long-distance runner and the 100-yard dash man. The trumpeter in the orchestra usually tires because of occasional short bursts of exertion. The band cornettist becomes exhausted by a slower plodding along. In both cases the player must take his special circumstances into consideration so that he may rely on his endurance to see him through to the last note of the programme.

Teaching traditions, study methods, playing experience, and the similarity of the instruments somehow have led most players of both the cornet and the trumpet to accept more or less the same concepts of tone and style of playing. This is unfortunate. In a 50-piece concert band where maybe there are, or should be, 5 cornets and 2 trumpets, the composers and players should both somehow take advantage of the two instruments, and write and play accordingly. A really good band concert can surely be just as musically rewarding as a fine orchestral programme—provided that the band does not attempt to play the same repertoire and style and relies more on its distinctiveness as a wind ensemble.

A REPERTOIRE LIST

It is an unfortunate fact that, compared to the other instruments of the orchestra, and excepting contemporary literature, there is really not much solo (and chamber music with parts for trumpet) literature for the trumpet that is of much worth. And it seems that just about every time a trumpeter is invited to perform a solo with the orchestra, he is requested to play the Haydn Concerto. There are some valid reasons for this state of affairs. As I pointed out in the first chapter, in Baroque and pre-Baroque music there was no chromatic trumpet. The most popular cup-mouthpiece wind instruments of those periods were the old 'cornett' and the long Baroque trumpet. Our modern trumpet and cornet arrived on the musical scene quite late in comparison to other orchestral instruments; and even after the invention of the valve, it was several decades before manufacturers could provide us with an instrument with fair intonation and a uniform tone quality throughout its whole range which was technically capable of solo work. Of course, the characteristic trumpet tone limits to some extent its use in chamber music, as it can be, especially in not-too-capable hands, quite overbearing when playing with, for instance, a string or woodwind ensemble. In spite of these facts, however, it is well known that such composers as Bach and Handel and Purcell and many Italian and English Baroque composers wrote superbly for an instrument certainly not as 'playable' as that which we have today. And with regard to chamber music, contemporary composers such as Stravinsky and Hindemith wrote very well for the modern trumpet in combination with other instruments.

Another element which enters into this is the fact that many early solo performers on the newly-arrived brass instruments were too eager to show off their virtuoso talents at the expense of their music. Even today there are several very capable trumpeters and cornettists who are still playing the old 'war-horse' theme-and-variation type solos popular a half-century ago. This has permeated into the concert band repertoire to the point where one finds little solo literature of merit. Thus, though there are hundreds of such solos available, and though I believe them to be invaluable to the student as training pieces, I have not included them in the following repertory list.

The chapters of this book on technique were designed with the hopes that students of all abilities might find some useful hints and aids to their study. However, the works listed in the repertoire list are mainly in the 'medium-difficult' to the 'very difficult' category and most of them can only be attempted by advanced students of the trumpet. They are mostly concert and recital pieces; not training studies. This list of course does not pretend to be a complete bibliography of trumpet solo works, and represents mainly the author's personally favoured trumpet works. I have not included many transcriptions except in certain cases where the trumpet works extremely well and where the character of the piece obviously suggests that of the trumpet. Unlisted also are the many excellent oratorios and cantatas of both Bach and Handel in which the trumpet is used as a solo instrument. I have included a few works for the standard orchestral repertoire in which the trumpet is used in an important solo capacity.

Most of the works listed under 'Trumpet and Orchestra' are available in piano score editions. When publishers are not shown the work probably exists only in manuscript.

Abbreviations

picc	piccolo	vl	violin
fl	flute	vla	viola
ob	oboe	vc	cello
cl	clarinet	db	double bass
bn	bassoon	pf	piano
hn	french horn	tym	tympani
trpt	trumpet	perc	percussion
cnt	cornet	tamb	tambourine
trb	trombone	sn. dr	snare drum
org	organ	vib	vibraphone
cel	celeste	gtr	guitar
hp	harp	al. sax	alto saxophone
WW	woodwind	ten. sax	tenor saxophone
cont	continuo	4tet	quartet
strgs	strings	5tet	quintet
sopr	soprano	bar	baritone horn
chor	chorus	euph	euphonium
eng. hn	English horn (cor anglais)	cymb	cymbal
tba	tuba		

Contents list

Solo trumpet
Trumpet and piano

Trumpet in Chamber Music:
2 players

Trumpet and organ	3 players
Trumpet and orchestra	4 players
2–4 Trumpets and orchestra	5 players
Trumpet ensemble	6 players
	7 players
	8 players
	9 players
	10 or more players

Solo trumpet

ADLER, SAMUEL: Canto I (*OUP*)
ARNOLD, MALCOLM: Fantasy (*Faber*)
CAMPO: Times, Op. 39 (*WIM*)
GREEN, GEORGE: Triptych (1971) (*Ph*)
KETTING: Intrada (*Don*)
SOMMERFELDT: Divertimento for Trpt., op. 21 (*Nors*)
TULL: 8 Profiles (*B & H*)

Trumpet and piano

ANDRÉ-BLOCH: Meou-tan-yin (1939) (*Gras*)
ANTHEIL, GEORGE: Sonata (1953) (*Wein*)
ARUTINIAN: Concerto (*Int*)
ASAFIEV, BORIS: Sonata (*King*)
AUBAIN, JEAN: Marche et Scherzo (1958) (*Led*)
BARAT, J. E.: Andante et Scherzo (1926) (*Led*); Fantaisie en mi bémol
    (1929) (*Led*); Lento et Scherzo (*Led*)
BARILLER, ROBERT: Citoyen Mardi-Gras (1952) (*Led*)
BEAUCAMP, ALBERT: Arlequinade (1949) (*Led*)
BEDOUIN, PAUL: Fantaisie (1947) (*Led*)
BENTZON, NIELS: Sonata, Op. 73 (*HanW, Chester*)
BERGHMANS, JOSE: La Chenille (1958) (*Led*)
BEVERSDORF: Sonata (*Southern*)
BIGOT, EUGÈNE: Elegie et Bourrée (*Led*)
BITSCH, MARCEL: Capriccio (1952) (*Led*); Fantaisietta (1950) (*Led*;
    Four Variations on a Theme of Scarlatti (1950) (*Led*)
BODA: Sonatina (*Southern*)
DE BOECK (b. 1865): Allegro de Concours (*Fisc*)
BOHRNSTEDT: Concerto (1953) (*War*)
BONDON, JACQUES: Concert de Printemps (1958) (*EdMa*)
BONNEAU: Suite (1944) (*Led*)
LE BOUCHER, MAURICE: Scherzo Appassionata (1933) (*Led*)
BOURNONVILLE: Pendant la Fête (1929) (*Cost*)

BOZZA, EUGÈNE: Badinage (1942) (*Led*); Caprice (1943) (*Led*);
   Rustiques (*Led*)
BRANDT: Zweites Konzertstück in Eb Major (*Zim, Novello*)
BUSSER, H. P.: Andante et Scherzo (1911) (*Led*); Variations in Eb
   (*Led*)
CASTERÈDE, J.: Brèves recontres (*Led*); Sonatine (1956) (*Led*)
CHALLAN, HENRI: Variations (1959) (*Led*)
CHEVREUILLE, R.: Concerto (*CBDM*)
CLERGUE: Sarabande et Rigaudon (1936) (*Lem*)
CONSTANT, MARIUS: Trois mouvements (1960) (*Led*)
CORDS, GUSTAV (b. 1870) Konzert-Fantaisie (*Schmi*)
CORELLI, A. (1653–1713): Sonata VIII (*Pr*)
DALLIER: Fête Joyeuse (1905) (*Led*)
DAMASE, J-M. (b. 1928): Hymne (*Lem*)
DEFAYE: Sonatine (*Led*)
DEFOSSEZ (b. 1905): Récitative et Allégro (*Gerv*)
DELAMS, MARC-JEAN: Chorale et Variations, Op. 37 (1914) (*Andr*)
DONATO, ANTHONY: Prélude et Allégro (1958) (*Led*)
DUBOIS, THÉODORE: Fantaisie (1920) (*Led*); Petit piston deviendra
   grand (*Led*)
EMMANUEL, MAURICE: Sonate (1937) (*Led*)
ENESCO, GEORGES: Légende (1906) (*Int*)
FLOTHUIS, M. H. (b. 1914): Aria, Op. 18 (*Don*)
FRANÇAIX, JEAN: Sonatina (1952) (*Esc*)
FRIBOULET, GEORGES: Introduction et Marche (1958) (*Lem*)
GABAYE: Boutade (*Led*); Feu d'artifice (*Led*); Sonatine (*Led*)
GAUBERT, P.: Cantabile et Scherzetto (1909) (*Led*)
GOEDICKE, A. (b. 1877): Concert Etude, Op. 49 (*M & M*)
GOEYENS, A.: Fantaisie Dramatique (*Bel*); Morceau de Concours
   (1945) (*Brog*); Introduction et Scherzo (*Fisc*)
GOTKOVSKY: Concertino (*Sal*)
HAMILTON, I.: 5 Scenes (1966) (*Pr*)
HILLEMACHER, P.: 1st Solo (1897) (*Led*)
HINDEMITH, P.: Sonata für Trompete (1939) (*As*)
HONEGGER: Intrada (1947) (*Sal*)
HUBEAU: Sonate (1944) (*Dur*)
HUMMEL, B.: Sonatine (1965) (*Benj, Schauer*)
IBERT, JACQUES: Impromptu (1951) (*Led*)
JONGEN, J.: Concertino (1913) (*Brog*)
JONGEN, L.: Air et Danse (1960) (*Lem*)
KENNAN, KENT: Sonata (1956) (*War*)
KOETSIER: Sonatina (*Don*)
KUPFERMAN, MEYER: Three Ideas (1967) (*Gen*)
LAURIDSEN, MORTEN: Sonata (1973) (*King*)

LONGINOTTI, P.: Scherzo Iberico (1942) (*Henn*)
MALIPIERO: Le fanfaron de la fanfare (*Led*)
MARTINŮ, B. (1890–1959): Sonatine (*Led*)
MAYER, WM.: Concert Piece (*B & H*)
MONTBRUN: Sarabande et Finale (1949) (*Led*)
MOUQUET: Impromptu (*Led*)
NERUDA, J.: Concerto in Eb (*MusR*)
PEASLEE: Nightsongs (*Eur*)
PEETERS, FLOR: Sonate, Op. 51 (1945) (*Pete*)
PETIT, A.: Etude de Concours (*Fisc*)
PILSS, KARL: Sonate für Trompete (1935) (*UE*)
POOT, MARCEL: Etude de Concert (1929) (*Esc*)
PORRINO, E. (1910–59): Prelude, Aria, Scherzoi in F (*SuvZ*)
ROBBINS: Mont St. Michel (*Led*)
RUEFF, J.: Fantasie Concertante (*Led*); Sonatine (1957) (*Led*)
SAINT-SAËNS, C.: Fantaisie en mi bémol (1935) (*Led*)
SAVARD, M.: Morceau de Concours (1909) (*Fisc*)
SCHOENBACH, DIETER: Konzert nach Scarlatti (*Mue*)
SHAPERO, H.: Sonata for C Trpt. (1956) (*SoNY*)
STEVENS, HALSEY (B, 1908): Sonata (*Pete*)
SUTERMEISTER, H.: Gavotta de Concert (*Sche*)
TOMASI, H. F.: Triptyque (1957) (*Led*)
VACHEY: Sonatine (*Del*)
VITTORIA: Chanson et Danse (1961) (*Led*)
WORMSER: Fantaisie, Thème et Variations (*Led*)
WUORINEN, C.: Nature's Concord (1972) (*Pete*)

Trumpet and organ

ALBINONI, T. (1671–1750): Concert en Fa (*Bill*)
ANDROVENDINI (1665–1707): Sonata No. 3 for 2 Trpts. (*Int*)
GAGNEBIN, H.: Sonata (*SchL*)
HOVHANESS, A.: Prayer of St. Gregory (*SoNY*); Sonata (1963) (*Pete*)
LANGLAIS, J.: Pièce pour Trompette (1972) (*EdPh*)
MOURET, JEAN (1682–1738): Sinfonies de Fanfares (*Gray*)
PURCELL, H. (1659–95): Ceremonial Music (*Pr*)
SOMMERFELDT: Elegy, Op. 27 (*Nors*)
STANLEY (1713–86): Suite No. 1 (*BrP*)
TELEMANN, G. (1681–1767): 3 Airs (*Bel*)
TOMASI, HENRI: Variations Grégoriennes (1964) (*Led*)
TORELLI, G. (1658–1709): Concertino in C Major (*Int*)
VERACINI, F. (1685–1750): Concerto en mi mineur (*Bill*); Sonate (*Bill*)
VIVIANI: Two Sonatas (*MusR*)

Trumpet and orchestra

ADDISON, J.: Concerto for Trpt (1951) (*Will, Stainer & Bell*)

ALBINONI (1671–1750): Concerto in D minor (*Bill*)

ALBRECHTSBERGER, J.: Concertino for Trpt in E♭ (1771) (*EdMB*)

ALGRIMM, HANS: Konzert in F dur (1938) *Lei*)

ARUTUNIAN, ALEX: Concerto (1967) (*Int*)

BACH, J. S. (1685–1750): Brandenburg Concerto No. 2 in F Major for F trpt, fl, ob, vn, strgs, ceb. (*KalA*)

BARSANTI, FRANCESCO (1690–1760): Concerto Grosso, Op. 3 No. 10 for trpt, 2 ob, strgs, cont. (*Eul*)

BERGHMANS, JOSE: Concerto grosso for trpt, hn, trb, strg. orch, perc. (*Led*)

BIBER, HENRICO (1644–1704) Sonata a6 (*MusR*)

BLOCHER, BORIS: Concerto for Winds, Harp and Strg. Orch. (*Bote*)

BLOCH, ERNST: Proclamation for Trpt and Orch. (1956) (*BroB*)

BOND, CAPEL: Trumpet Concerto (1760) (*B & H*)

BONNEAU: Fantaisie Concertante (1950) (*Led*)

BORDES, C.: Divertissement (1915) (*Baro*)

BRENTA, GASTON: Concertino (1958) (*Led*)

BREUER, KARL: atonalyse II (1959) (*Siko*)

CHARLIER: Solo de Concours (1943) (*Lem*)

CHAYNES, CHARLES: Concerto (1956) (*Led*)

CHEVREUILLE, RAYMOND: Concerto (1954) (*CBDM*)

CLARKE, JEREMIAH (c.1674–1707): Trumpet Voluntary; Suite in D Major (*MusR*)

COPLAND, AARON: Quiet City for trpt, eng hn, strgs. (1941) (*B & H*)

CORELLI: Sonata for Trumpet, Violins and Basso Continuo (*MusR*)

DELERUE, G.: Concertino (1951) (*Led*)

DESENCLOS: Incantation, Thrène, et Danse (1953) (*Led*)

DESPORTES: Concerto (1949) (*And*)

DUBOIS, PIERRE: Concertino (1959) (*Led*)

FASCH, JOHANN F. (1688–1758): Concerto in D Major (*Siko*)

GABAYE, PIERRE: Feu d'artifice (1964) (*Led*)

GABRIELI, DOMENICO (1659–90) Trumpet Sonata (*MusR*)

GIANNINI: Concerto (1948) (*Rem*)

GIBBONS, ORLANDO (1583–1625): Suite for Trumpet and Strings (*Will*)

GOTKOVSKY, I.: Concerto (1973) (*EdMT*)

HANDEL, G. F. (1685–1759): Tromba Suite (*Hin*); The Trumpet Shall Sound: *Messiah*

HANSON, RAYMOND: Concerto

HAYDN, JOSEF (1732–1809): Concerto for Trumpet (1796) (*B & H*)

HAYDN, MICHAEL (1737–1806): Trompeten Konzert in D dur (*Bill*)

HUMMEL, JOHANN N. (1778–1837): Trumpet Concerto (1796) (*Bill*)

HINDEMITH, PAUL: Concerto for trpt, bn, and String Orch. (1949) (*SchM*)

HOROVITZ, JOSEPH: Concerto for trpt and orchestra (1963) (*Nov*)

IBERT, JACQUES: Divertissement pour Orchestre de Chambre (1930) (*Dur*)

IVES, CHARLES: The Unanswered Question (1908) for trpt, 4 fl., strgs. (*SouT*)

JACCHINI, GIUSEPPI (fl. 17th–18th cent.): Sonata No. 5 in D Major (*MusR*)

JOLIVET, ANDRÉ: Concertino (1948) (*Dur*)

KAMINSKI, JOSEPH: Concertino for Trumpet (1952) (*Is*)

KOX, HANS: Concertante Muziek for trpt, hn, trb, orch. (1956) (*Don*)

LOEILLET, J.: Concerto in D Major (*Bill*)

LOUCHEUR, RAYMOND: Concertino (1962) (*Sal*)

LOVELOCK: Concerto (*SoNY*)

MARTIN, FRANK: Concerto pour 7 instruments: wind, perc. & strgs (1949) (*UE*)

MAYER, WM.: Concert Piece (1959) (*B & H*)

MILHAUD, DARIUS: Symphonie Concertante for trpt, bn, hn, cb, orch. (1959) (*Heu*)

MOLTER, JOHANN-MELCHIN (1696–1765): Concerto No. 2 in D Major (*MusR*)

MOZART, LEOPOLD (1719–87): Concerto for D Trumpet (1762) (*Kis*)

MUDGE, RICHARD (1718–63): Trumpet Concerto (1760) (*MusR*)

NERUDA, J.: Concerto in E♭ (*MusR*)

PAKHMUTOVA, ALEXANDRA: Concerto in E♭ minor (*USSR*)

PANUFNIK, ANDREZEJ: Concerto in modo antico for trpt, hp, strgs, tym (1956) (*B & H*)

PEASLEE, RICHARD: Nightsongs (1974) (*Hel, p. 499*)

PERSICHETTI, V.: The Hollow Men (1948) (*EV*)

PILSS, KARL: Concerto (1934) (*As*)

PLANEL, R.: Concerto (1973) (*EdMT*)

PORRINO: Concertino (1936) (*And*)

PURCELL, HENRY: Trumpet Overture from *The Indian Queen* (1695); Sonata for Trumpet and Strings; Duke of Gloucester's Birthday Ode (*MusR*)

RESPIGHI, O.: Concerto a cinque for trpt, ob, vl, cb, pf, strgs (1934) (*RicL*)

RIISAGER: Concertino, Op. 29 (1935) (*HanW*)

ROGER, KURT G.: Concerto grosso No. 1 for solo trpt, tym, strgs (1954) (*Che*)

ROSIER, CARL (1640–1725): Sonata for trumpet, strings and continuo (*Schw*)

SCARLATTI (1660–1725): Su le sponde del Tebro: cantata (voce sola con violini et tromba) (*SM*)

SCHOENBACH, DIETER: Konzert for trumpet and chamber orchestra (*SM*)

SCRIABIN: Poem of Ecstasy (1908)

SHOSTAKOVICH: Concerto for Piano, Trumpet and Strings Op. 35 (1933) (*BroB*)

SPERGER, J. M.: Konzert in D dur (1779) (*HofL*)

STANLEY, JOHN (1713–86): Trumpet Tune (*OUP*)

STARER, R.: Invocation (1962) (*Bel*)

STEKKE, LEON: Concerto, Op. 17 (1937) (*Brog*)

STOEZEL: Concerto in D Major (*Bill*)

STRADELLA, ALESSANDRO (1642–82): Sonata for trpt. & 2 string orchestras (*King*)

TARTINI, G. (1692–1770): Concerto in C Major (*Bill*)

TELEMANN, G. P.: Konzert in D dur for trpt, strings, continuo (*Siko*)

THILMAN, JOHANNES: Concertino für Trompete, Op. 66 (1956) (*Hof*)

TOMASI, HENRI: Concerto (1948) (*Led*)

TORELLI, G.: Concerto in D Major (*Int*); Sinfonia con Tromba (*King*)

TULL, FISHER: Concerto No. 2 (1978) (*B & H*)

VASILENKO, C.: Concerto, Op. 113 (*Leed*)

VEJVANOWSKI, PAVEL (1640–93): Sonata a4 for Trpt & Strings (Musica Antiqua Bohemia) (*Art*)

VERACINI, F. M. (1690–1768): Concerto in E minor (*Bill*)

WAL-BERG: Concerto (1948) (*Leed*)

ZBINDEN, JULIEN: Concertino pour Trompète et Orchestre (1959) (*SchL*)

2–4 trumpets and orchestra

ANDRIESSEN, J. (b. 1925): Symphonietta Concertante 4 trpts, orch. (*Don*)

BACH, J. S.: Orchestral Suite No. 3 in D 3 trpts, 2 ob, perc, strgs, cont.; Orchestral Suite No. 4 in D 3 trpts, 3 ob, perc, strgs, cont.; Christmas Oratario; B Minor Mass (*Pete*)

BONONCINI, GIOVANNI (1670–1747): Sinfonia decima a 7 solo instrs. (*MusR*)

CORELLI: Concertino (*SchM*)

EDER, H.: Musik für 2 Trompeten und Streichorchester, Op. 23 (1961) (*BH-W*)

FRANCESCHINI, PETRONIO: Sonata in D 2 trpts, strgs (1680) (*MusR*)

HANDEL, G. F.: *Judas Maccabaeus* (1747); Music for the Royal Fireworks

JACCHINI, G.: Sonata Op. 5 for 2 trpts (*MusR*)

KETTING, OTTO: Concertino for 3 trpts, orch. (*Don*)

LEGRENZI, GIOVANNI (1626–90): Sonata 'La Buscha' 2 trpts, strgs, cont. (*MusR*)

MANFREDINI, FRANCESCO (c. 1680–1748): Concerto per due Trombe (*Car*)

MARTINI, PADRE: Sonata for 4 Trumpets & Strgs (1743) (*King*)

MOLTER, J-M. (1696–1765): Concerto 2 trpts, orch. (*MusR*)

PERTI, GIACOMO (1661–1756): Sonata for 4 Trpts, Strgs (*MS*)

PURCELL, HENRY: Yorkshire Feast Song: Symphony 3 trpts, strgs, tym, cont. (1690); Voluntary in C for 2 trpts; The Cebell for 2 trpts, strgs, perc, cont. (1692); Symphony from *The Fairy Queen* for 2 trpts, strgs, tym. (*Merc*)

PURCELL, DANIEL (1660–1717): Sonata for 2 trpts, orch. (*SchM*)

STRADELLA, A. (1642–82): Sonata a4 2 trpts, strgs, with trb. (*Cost*)

TELEMANN, G. P.: Concerto No. 1 for 3 trpts, tym, 2 ob, strgs (*MusR*)

TORELLI, G.: Sinfonia in D for 2 trpts, strgs, cont. (*Siko*); Sinfonia in D for 2 ob, 2 trpts (*MS*); Sinfonia for 4 trpts, ob, strgs, tym. (*MusR*)

VEJVANOWSKY, PAVEL: Sonata Venatorio for 2 trpts and strgs (1684) (Musica Antiqua Bohemica, Vol. 2); Serenada for 2 trpts and strgs (1670) (*Art*)

VIVALDI, ANTONIO (1669–1741): Concerto in E♭ for 2 trpts; Concerto in C for 2 trpts (*Int*)

Trumpet ensemble
(unaccompanied unless marked)

ALTENBURG, JOHANN (1736–1801): Concerto for Clarini and Tym. (7 trpts, tym.) (*King*)

ARNOLD, HUBERT: Sonata for 2 trpts and pf. (*SouT*)

BACH, C. P. E. (1714–88): March (Fanfare) 3 trpts, tym. (*Mark*)

BACH, J. S.: *Easter Cantata*: My Spirit be Joyful 2 trpts, organ (*Merc*); Two Fanfares & Chorale 3 trpts, organ (*As*)

BOZZA, EUGENE (b. 1905): Dialogue for 2 trpts (*Led*)

BRITTEN, B. (1913–76): Fanfare for St. Edmundsbury: 3 trpts (*B & H*)

CASTERÈDE, J.: 6 Pièces brèves en duo (*Led*)

DAQUIN, LOUIS C. (1694–1772): Noel Suisse 3 trpts, organ (*King*)

ERB, K. (1877–1958): Diversions for 2 trpts and pf. (*Pr*)

FRESCOBALDI, GIROLAMO (1583–1643): Canzona a due for 2 trpts, organ, cont. (*SchM*)

HOVHANESS, A. (b. 1911): Khaldis for 4 trpts, perc, pf. (*King*)

LASSUS, ORLANDUS (1532–94): Providebam Dominum 3 trpts, organ (*King*)

LEVY, ERNST: Fanfares for 3 trpts (1947) (*BroB*)

MARC-CARLES: Danses dans le Style Ancien for 2 trpts. (1963) (*Led*)

MUCZYNSKI, R.: Trumpet Trio, Op. 11 (1961) (*SchG*)

OSBORNE, WILLSON: Four Fanfares based on 18th-century French Hunting Calls (1958) (*King*)

PHILLIPS, BURRILL: Trio for Trumpets (1937) (*King*)

PINKHAM, DANIEL (b. 1923): Te Deum for 3 trpts, org, chor. (*King*)

PLOG: Contemporary Music for 2 trpts (*Wimb*)

PURCELL, HENRY: Ceremonial Music for 2 trpts, organ (*Merc*)

REYNOLDS, VERNE: Music for 5 Trumpets (*King*)

SCHEIDT, SAMUEL (1587–1654) Canzon for 4 Trumpets (*King*)

STEIN, LEON: Trio for 3 Bb trpts (*Pr*)

TELEMANN, G. P.: Heroic Music for 2 trpts, organ (*Int*)

TOMASI, H. F. (1901–71) Suite for 3 trpts (*Led*)

Trumpet in chamber music

For two players

BRAAL, ANDRIES: L'illumination de Queekhoven (1968) trpt, harp (*Don*)

BAZELOR: Double Crossings (1976) trpt, perc. (*B & H*)

BORDEN, DAVID: Fifteen dialogues for trpt, trb, (1962) (*Ens*)

BOZZA, EUGENE: Quatre Esquisses (1974) trpt, trb (*Led*)

DIJK, J. VAN: Serenade for trpt, hn (*Don*)

KRAFT, W.: Encounters III trpt, pc (*WIM*)

LEONARD: Fanfare and Allegro trpt, tym (*Benj*)

For three players

ARDEVOL, JOSE: Tercera Sonata a Tres (1945) 2 trpts, trb (*IIM*)

BIALOSKY: Two Movements for Brass Trio (1954) trpt, hn, trb (*King*)

BLACHER, BORIS: Divertimento Op. 131 (1958) trpt, trb, pf (*Bote*)

CASTERÈDE, J.: Concertino (1959) trpt, trb, pf (*Led*)

FLOTHUIS, M.: Sonatina, Op. 26 trpt, hn, trb (*Don*)

GLASSER, STANLEY: Trio for 2 trpts & trb (1958) (*MusR*)

GOEB, ROGER: Suite trpt, fl, cl (*King*)

HANDEL, G. F.: Let the Bright Seraphim trpt, sop, pf (*Tro*)

HOUDY, P.: Divertissement (1956) trpt, hn, pf (*Led*)

KNIGHT, MORRIS: Cassation (1962) trpt, hn, trb (*Tri*)

LECLERCQ, EDGARD: Suite Classique trpt, hn, trb (*Brog*)

LOUEL, JEAN: Trio (1956) trpt, hn, trb (*ElkH*)

MAREK, R.: Trio for Brass Instruments (1959) trpt, hn, trb (*King*)

MEULEMANS, ARTHUR (b. 1884) Trio trpt, hn, trb (*CBDM*)

PINKHAM, D.: Brass Trio trpt, hn, trb (*Pete*)

POULENC, FRANCIS (1899–1963): Sonata trpt, hn, trb (*Che*)

QUINET, MARCEL: Sonate à trois (1961) trpt, hn, trb (*CBDM*)

SANDERS, R.: Trio (1961) trpt, hn, trb (*King*)

SCHARRES, CHARLES: Divertimento (1958) trpt, hn, trb (*Brog*)

SCHISKE, KARL (1916–69): Musik für Clarinette, Trompete und Bratsche (viola), Op. 27 (*UE*)

SURINACH, C. (b. 1915) Ritmo Jondo (flamenco) trpt, cl, pc (*As*)

SUTERMEISTER, H. (b. 1910): Serenade I trpt, 2 cls, bn (*SchM*)

For four players

ADDISON, J. (b. 1920): Divertimento, Op. 9 2 trpts, hn, bar (*Bel*)

ANDRIESSEN, HENDRIK (b. 1892): Aubade 2 trpts, hn, trb (*Don*)

ANDRIESSEN, JURRIAAN: Introduzione e allegro (1958) 2 trpts, hn, trb (*Don*)

ANTEGNATI: Canzon 9 2 trpts, 2 trb (*MusR*)

BERGER: Intrada 2 trpts, 2 trb (*King*)

BERGSMA, W. (b. 1921): Suite for Brass Quartet 2 trpts, trb, bar (*Fisc*)

BOEDIJN, G. (b. 1893): Quartet 2 trpts, hn, trb (*Don*)

BROOKS, ALFREDO: Cuarteto no. 3. Op. 31 (1919) trpt, vl, vc, pf (*BH-W*)

CASELLA, ALFREDO: Sinfonia, Op. 54 (1933) trpt, cl, vc, pf (*Car*)

CHAVEZ, CARLOS: Soli (1933) trpt, ob, cl, bn (*B & H*)

DELANNOY, MARCEL: Rapsodie (1934) trpt, al. sax, vc, pf (*Heu*)

FRANKENPOHL, ARTHUR: Quartet (1950) 2 trpts, trb, bar (*King*)

FRESCOBALDI, G.: Canzon 13 2 trpts, 2 trbs (*MusR*)

GABAYE, P.: Recreation trpt, hn, trb, pf (*Led*)

GABRIELI, ANDREA (1520–86): Ricercar del sesto tuono 2 trpts, 2 trb (*MusR*)

GABRIELI, GIOVANNI (1554–1612): Canzona per Sonaro Nos. 1–4 2 trpts, 2 trb (*King*)

GLASEL (ed.): 16th-century Carmina 2 trpts, 2 trb (*Cham*)

HAINES, EDMUND: Toccata 2 trpts, 2 trb (*King*)

HEISS, HERMANN: Trompetenmusik (1934) 2 trpts, 2 trb (*BH-W*)

HINDEMITH, PAUL (1895–1963): Morgenmusik 2 trpts, 2 trb (*SchM*)

HOVHANESS, A.: Sharagan and Fugue 2 trpts, 2 trb (*King*)

IPUCHE-RIVA, PEDRO: Primera Serie de Productos Quimicos C trpt, fl, cl, bn (*L-AM*)

JACOB, GORDON (1895–1984): Scherzo 2 trpts, hn, bar (*Len*)

KAY, ULYSSES: Brass Quartet (1958) 2 trpts, 2 trb (*Peer*)

KELLER, HOMER: Quartet (1954) 2 trpts, hn, trb (*King*)

KETTING, O. (b. 1935): Sonata 2 trpts, hn, trb. (*Don*)

KLEIN, JOHN: Sonata (1950) 2 trpts, 2 trb (*As*)

LEWALLEN, JAMES: Quartet (1952) trpt, cnt, trb, bar (*MS*)

MOLTER, J. M.: Concerti a4 in D Major trpt, 2 ob, bn (*MusR*)

OBRECHT, JACOB: Tsat een meskin (1950) trpt, 3 trb (*King*)

PEETERS, F.: Entrata Festiva 2 trpts, hn, trb (*Pete*)

PITTALUGA, GUSTAVO: Ricercare (1934) trpt, vn, cl, bn (*Led*)

PURCELL, HENRY: Music for Queen Mary II 2 trpts, 2 trb (*King*)

RAMSOE, W.: 4 Quartets (1888) 2 trpts, hn, tba (*HanW*)

RATTENBACH, AUGUSTOS: Serenata (1966) C trpt, fl, cl, vc (*Peer*)

REICHE, GOTTFRIED: Sonatas from Neue Quatricinia trpt, hn, trb, tba (*King*)

REIGGER, WALLINGFORD: Movement for 2 trpts, trb, pf Op. 66 (1960) (*Peer*)

ROLAND-MANUEL: Suite dans le goût español trpt, ob, bn, harpsichord (1938) (*Dur*)

SANDERS, ROBERT.: Suite (1956) 2 trpts, 2 trb (*King*)

SHEINKMAN, M.: Divertimento (1957) trpt, cl, trb, hp (*Pete*)

SUTERMEISTER, H.: Serenade (1956) trpt, 2 cl, bn (*SchM*)

TELEMANN, G. P.: Konzert in D dur trpt, 2 ob, cont (*Siko*)

VAN PRAAG, HENRI: Sonate (1950) 2 trpt, hn, trb (*Don*)

For five players

ANON.: Sonata from Bankelsängerlieder (1624) 2 trpts, hn, trb, tba (*King*)

ANTEGNATI: Canzon 20 (1608) 2 trpts, 3 trb (*MusR*)

BACH, J. S.: Contrapunctus I 2 trpts, hn, 2 trb (*King*)

BARON, SAMUEL (arr.): Impressions of a Parade 2 trpts, hn, trb, tba (*SchG*)

BOZZA, EUGENE (b. 1905): Sonatine 2 trpts, hn, trb, tba (*Led*)

BROWN, E.: Pastorale trpt, trb, fl, cl, alto sax (*See*)

CASELLA, ALFREDO: Serenata (1927) trpt, cl, bn, vl, vc (*UE*)

CONSTANT, M. (b. 1925): 4 Etudes de Concert trpt, 2 hns, trb, perc (*Led*)

DAHL, INGOLF: Music for Brass Instruments (1944) 2 trpts, hn, 2 trb, opt. tba (*Wit*)

EWALD, VICTOR: Symphony for Brass (1911) 2 trpts, hn, 2 trb, opt. tba (*King*)

GABRIELI, GIOVANNI: Canzona prima a5 2 trpts, hn, trb, tba (*Men*); Sonata pian' e forte 2 trpts, 2 trb, org. (*King*)

HANDEL, G. F.: Overture to *Berenice* 2 trpts, hn, 2 trb (*King*)

HARRIS, ARTHUR: Four Moods for Brass Quintet (1957) 2 trpts, hn, trb, tba (*Men*)

HERTEL, JOHANN W. (1727–89):Concerto à Cinque trpt, 2 ob, 2 bn (*Noe*)

HINDEMITH, PAUL: Drei Stücke für fünf Instrumente (1934) trpt, cl, vl, cb, pf (*SchM*); Tafelmusik from *Plönermusiktag* (1932) trpt, fl, 2 vl, vc (*SchM*)

HOLBORNE, ANTHONY (d. 1602): Three Pieces 2 trpts, hn, trb, tba (*Men*); Two Pieces 2 trpts, hn, 2 trb (*King*)

KOETSIER: Brass Quintet 2 trpts, hn, trb, tba (*Don*)

LOCKE, M. (1632–77): Music for His Majesty's Sackbuts and Cornetts 2 trps, 3 trb (*OUP*)

LOCKWOOD, NORMAND (b. 1906): Concerto for Organ and Brass 2 trpts, 2 trb, organ (*As*)

MONNIKENDAM, MARIUS (b. 1896): Concerto 2 trpts, 2 trb, organ (*Don*)

MÜLLER-ZURICH, PAUL: *Ein feste Burg*, Choral Toccata Op. 54 No. 1 (1956) 2 trpt, 2 trb, organ; *Wie schon leuchet der Morgenstern* Op. 54 No. 2 (1956) 2 trpt, 2 trb, organ (*BA*)

NAGEL, ROBERT: Suite for Brass and Piano trpt, hn, trb, tba, pf (*Men*)

PEUERL, P. (c. 1570–1625): Canzoni No. 1 and 2 2 trpts, hn, trb, tba; Suite 2 trpts, hn, trb, tba (*Pr*)

PEZEL, JOHANN: Fünff-stimmigte bläsende Music (1685) 2 trpts, hn, trb, tba; Hora decima (1670) 2 trpts, hn, trb, tba (*King*)

PILSS, K.: Capriccio 2 trpts, hn, 2 trb; Scherzo 3 trpts, 2 trb (*King*)

POWELL, MEL (b. 1923): Divertimento trpt, ob, fl, cl, bn (*Fisc*)

REVUELTAS. S. (1899–1940): First Little Serious Piece trpt, picc, ob, cl, bar. sax (*SoNY*)

REYNOLDS (ed.): Centones No. 1–8 2 trpts, hn, trb, tba (*SouT*); Suite for Brass Quintet 2 trpts, hn, trb, tba (*Bel*)

SANDERS, R.: Quintet in Bb (1948) 2 trpts, hn, 2 trb (*Fisc*)

SCHULLER, GUNTHER (b, 1925): Quintet 2 trpts, hn, trb, tba (*SchM*)

SOWERBY, LEO (1895–1968): Festival Musick 2 trpts, 2 trb, org (*SchG*)

STARER, R. (b. 1924): Five Miniatures for Brass Quintet (1952) 2 trpts, 2 hn, trb (*SoNY*)

SURINACH, CARLOS (b. 1915): Hollywood Carnival trpt, fl, cl, db, perc (*Rong*)

SWANSON, H. (b. 1899): Sound Piece 2 trpt, hn, trb, tba (*Wein*)

THOMSON, VIRGIL (b. 1896): Sonata da Chiesa trpt, Eb cl, hn, trb, vl (*NewM*)

TICE, DAVID: Four pieces for Brass Quartet & Tympani (1956) 2 trpts, 2 trb, tym (*Univ*)

WALTON, W. (1902–83): 6 Pieces Set II 2 trpts, 3 trb (*OUP*)

WASHBURN: Quintet 2 trpts, hn, trb, tba (*OUP*)

WHEAR, PAUL: Invocation & Study (1960) 2 trpts, hn, 2 trb (*King*)

ZINDARS, EARL: Quintet for Brass Instruments (1958) 2 trpts, hn, trb, tba (*King*); Quintet No. 2 2 trpts, hn, trb, tba (*Cam*)

For six players

ALBINONI, T.: Concerto in C trpt, 3 ob, bn, cont (*Siko*)

ARDEVOL, JOSE (b. 1911): Musica da Camera para 6 trpt, fl, cl, bn, vn, vc (*P-AU*)

AURIC, GEORGES: Five Bagatelles on Marlborough (1925) trpt, cl, bn, vn, vc, pf (*Heu*)

BOHME, OSKAR: Sextet, Op. 30 (1911) 2 trpts, hn, 2 trb, tba (*Wit*)

BUONAMENTE: Canzona a5 25 trpts, 3 trb, organ (*MusR*)

CONSTANT, MARIUS: Quatre Etudes de Concert (1957) trpt, 2 hn, trb, pf, perc (*Led*)

COWELL, HENRY (1897–1965): A Tall Tale 2 trpts, hn, 2 trb, tba (*Merc*)

IVES, CHARLES: Allegretto Sombreoso (1958) trpt, fl, 3 vn, pf (*Peer*)

KARG-ELERT, S.: Marche Triomphale 2 trpts, hn, trb, tba, organ (*Can*)

MARTINŮ, B.: *La Revue de cuisine*—(ballet fantastique) trpt, cl, bn, vl, vc, pf (*Led*)

MOLTER, J.-M.: Sinfonia Concertante trpt, 2 ob, 2 hn, bn (*MusR*)

MONTEUX, PIERRE (1875–1964): Deux piécettes trpt, fl, ob, cl, bn, perc (*Math*)

OSBORNE: Prelude 3 trpts, 3 trb; Two Ricercari 3 trpts, 3 trb (*King*)

OTTEN, LUDWIG: Cassation (1956) 3 trpts, 3 trb (*Don*)

RUGGLES, CARL: Angels (1939) 4 trpts, 2 trb (*Cur*)

SCHOENBERG, ARNOLD: Fünf geistliche Lieder, Op. 15 (1924) voice, trpt, fl, cl, hp, vl (*UE*)

SUTERMEISTER, H.: Serenade No. 2 trpt, hn, fl, ob, cl, bn (*SchM*)

WEBERN, ANTON: Fünf geistliche Lieder (1924) sopr, trpt, fl, cl, hp, vn (*UE*)

For seven players

BACH, J. S.: Ricercar 3 trpts, 4 trb (*King*)

BEREZOWSKY, NICOLAI (1900–53): Brass Suite, Op. 24 2 trpts, 2 hn, 2 trb, tba (*Bel*)

BOZZA, EUGENE: 4 Mouvements trpt, hn, trb, fl, ob, cl, bn (*Led*)

BUONAMENTE: Sonata 2 trpts, 2 hn, 2 trb, tba (*King*)

COHN, ARTHUR: Music for Brass Instruments(1950) 4 trpts, 3 trb (*SouT*)

COPPOLA, PIERO: 5 Poems (1933) trpt, fl, cl, 2 vl, vla, vc (*Dur*)

COWELL, HENRY (b. 1897): Rondo 3 trpts, 2 hn, 2 trb (*Pete*)

DAQUIN, L. C. (1694–1772): Noël Suisse 3 trpts, 3 trb, tba (*Tem*)

DUVERNOY, ALPHONSE (1842–1907): Serenade, Op. 24 trpt, 2 vl, vla, vc, cb, pf (*Heu*)

GOEB, ROGER: Septet for Brass Instruments (1952) 2 trpts, 2 hn, 2 trb, tba (*composer's facsimile edition*)

FRANCISQUE, ANTOINE: Suite from *Le Trésor d'Orphée* 2 trpts, 2 hn, 2 trb, bar (*King*)

HINDEMITH, PAUL: Septett (1948) trpt, fl, ob, b. cl, bn, hn (*SchM*)

HUMMEL, JOHANN: Military Septet, Op. 114 (1830) trpt, fl, cl, bn, vc, cb, pf (*Has*)

IBERT, JACQUES: Le Jardinier de Samos (1925) trpt, fl, cl, bn, vc, dr, tamb (*Heu*)

D'INDY, VINCENT: Suite dans le Style Ancien (1887) trpt, 2 fl, strg. 4tet (*Int*)

LASSUS, ORLANDUS (1532–94): Providebam Dominum 4 trpt, hn, 2 trb (*King*)

LOCKE, M.: Music for King Charles II 3 trpt, 3 trb, tba (*King*)

MARTINŮ, B.: Rondo (1950) trpt, ob, cl, bn, 2 vl, pf (*Art*)

MIROUZE, M.: Pièce en Septuor (1933) trpt, WW 5tet, pf (*Led*)

PIERNÉ, G. (1863–1937): Pastorale variée, Op. 30 trpt, fl, ob, cl, hn, 2 bn (*Dur*)

POPOV, GABRIELI: Septet, Op. 22 (1929) trpt, fl, cl, bn, vl, vc, db (*UE*)

SAINT-SAËNS, C.: Septet, Op. 65 trpt, 2 vn, vla, vc, db, pf (*Dur*)

SATIE, E. (1866–1925):Toute petite danse pour la piège de Méduse trpt, cl, trb, perc, vl, vc, db (*SchG*)

STRAVINSKY, I.: L'Histoire du Soldat (1918) cnt, cl, bn, trb, perc, vl, db (*Che*)

SYLVIUS, C.: Septet (1953) trpt, fl, ob, cl, bn, hn, trb (*Baro*)

WALTON, W.: Façade (1923) trpt, speaker, fl, cl, sax, vc, perc (*OUP*)

WYNER, Y. (b. 1929): Serenade trpt, cl, bn, trb, vl, vc, pf (*ACA*)

For eight players

ANGERER, P. (b. 1927): Quinta Ton 2 trpts, WW 5tet, trb (*UE*)

BONELLI, A.: Toccata (1602) 4 trpts, 4 trb (*King*)

BORRIS: Bläser-Oktett trpt, fl, ob, cl, b. cl, bn, 2 hns (*Hein*)

CODIVILLA, F: Octet (1919) cnt, fl, ob, cl, 2 hn, bn, trb (*Pizz*)

EL-DABH, HALIM (b. 1921): Thumaniya 2 trpts, fl, ob, cl, hn, 2 perc (*Pete*)

FELLEGARA, V.: Octet (1953) 2 trpts, WW 5tet, trb (*SuvZ*)

GABRIELI, GIOVANNI: Canzon primi Toni 4 trpts, 4 trb (*King*); Canzon septimi toni No. 1 4 trpts, 4 trb (*King*); Canzon septimi toni No. 2 4 trpts, 4 trb (*King*); Canzon noni toni 4 trpts, 4 trb (*King*); Sonata pian' e forte 4 trpts, 4 trb. (*King*); Canzon duodecima toni 4 trpts, 4 trb (*MusR*)

GAL, H.: Divertimento, Op. 22 (1924) trpt, fl, ob, 2 cl, 2 hn, bn (*Leu*)

HARSANYI, TIBOR: L'Histoire du petit tailleur (1950) trpt, fl, cl, bn, perc, vl, vc, pf (*Esc*)

HENZE, H. W.: Concerto per Il Marigny (1956) trpt, cl, b. cl. hn, trb, vla, vc, pf (*SchM*)

JACOB, GORDON: Interludes—from Music for a Festival (1955) 4 trpts, 3 trb, tym (*B & H*)

LESSARD, JOHN: Octet (1953) 2 trpts, fl, cl, bn, 2 hn, b. trb (*ACA*)

PASCAL, CLAUDE: Octet trpt, 2 fl, ob, cl, hn, 2 bn (*Dur*)

PINKHAM, D.: Christmas Cantata (1958) 4 trpts, 4 trb, chor (*King*)

REVUELTAS, S.: Toccata trpt, picc, E♭ cl, b. cl, hn, vl, tym (*SouT*)

SCHAT, PETER: Octet (1958) 2 trpt, fl, ob, cl, hn, bn, trb (*Don*)

SHAPEY, R. (b, 1921): Dimensions trpt, sop, fl, ob, ten. sax, hn, pf, db; (*Leeds*) Incantations trpt, sop, al. sax, hn, vc, pf, perc (*Leeds*)

SIMPSON, R.: Canzona for Brass (1958) 4 tripts, 3 trb, tba (*Len*)

STRAVINSKY, I.: Octet for Wind Instruments (1923) 2 trpts, fl, cl, 2 bn, 2 trb (*B & H*)

VARÈSE, EDGAR (1885–1965): Octandre (1924) trpt, WW 5tet, trb, db (*RicL*)

WAILLY, P. DE (1854–1933): Octet trpt, fl, ob, 2 cl, hn, 2 bn (*Rou*)

WALTON, W: A Queen's Fanfare 5 trpts, 3 trb (*OUP*)

ZILLIG, WINFRIED (b. 1905): Serenade I (1958) cnt, 2 trpts, 2 hn, 2 trb, tba (*BA*)

For nine players

CATURLA, A. G.: Primera suite cubana (1931) trpt, fl, ob, cl, b. cl, eng, hn, bn, hn, pf (*New Music Orchestra Series*)

FUX, JOHANN J. (1660–1741): Serenada a8 2 trpts, 2 ob, bn, 2 vl, vla, db (*Fel*)

GOOSSENS, E.: Fantasy Nonet, Op. 40 (1926) trpt, fl, ob, 2 cl, 2 hn, 2 bn (*Cur*)

IVES, CHARLES: La Pregunta incontestada (1941) trpt, 4 fl, 2 vl, vla, vc (*Peer*)

LUTYENS, E.: Chamber Concerto, Op. 8 No. 1 (1939) trpt, ob, cl, hn, bn, trb, vl, vla, vc (*Che*)

MILHAUD, DARIUS (1892–1974): Aspen Serenade C trpt, fl, cl, ob, bn, vl, vla, vc, db (*Heu*)

REVUELTAS, S.: Planos (1963) trpt, cl, b. cl, bn, 2 vls, vc, cb, pf (*SouT*)

RIEGGER, WALLINGFORD: Nonet for Brass (1951) 3 trpts, 2 hn, 3 trb, tba (*As*)

ROCHBERG, GEORGE: Chamber Symphony (1953) trpt, fl, cl, bn, hn, trb, vl, vla, vc (*Pr*)

SALVIUCCI, GIOVANNI: Serenata (1927) trpt, fl, ob, cl, bn, 2 vl, vla, vc (*Ric*)

WEBERN, ANTON: Concerto for Nine Instrs. Op. 24 (1934) trpt, fl, ob, cl, hn, trb, vl, vla, pf (*UE*); Two Songs, Op. 8 trpt, sopr, cl, hn, hp, cel, strg. trio (*UE*)

ZHIVOTOV, A. S.: Frammenti per nonetto Op. 2 (1930) trpt, fl, cl, bn, 2 vl, vla, vc, pf (*Mosc*)

ZILLIG, WINFRIED: Serenade II cnt, trpt, E♭ cl, A cl, b. cl, trb, vl, vla, vc (*BA*)

For ten or more players

ADLER, S.: Concert Piece 3 trpts, 2 hn, 3 trb, 2 bar, tba (*King*)

ANDRIESSEN, J.: Hommage à Milhaud trpt, hn, trb, fl, ob, cl, sax, bn, vl, vla, vc (*Don*); Rouw past Elektra 2 trpts, fl, 2 ob, cl, hn, 2 bn, 2 trb, tym, perc (*Don*)

ARNELL, R. (b. 1917): Ceremonial and Flourish 3 trpts, 4 hn, 3 trb (*As*)

BABBIT, M. (b. 1916): Music for Twelve Instruments trpt, WW 5tet, hp, cel, strg. trio, db (*Bom*)

BEADELL: Introduction and Allegro 3 trpts, 3 hn, 3 trb, bar, tba (*King*)

BEVERSDORF, TOM: Cathedral Music 3 trpts, 4 hn, 3 trb, bar, tba (*SouT*)

BONNEAU, P.: Fanfare 3 trpts, 3 hn, 2 trb, tba, tym (*Led*)

BOZZA, E. (b. 1905): Fanfare Hëroïque 3 trpts, 4 hn, 3 trb, tba, tym (*Led*)

CAZDEN, NORMAN: Concerto for 10 Instrs. Op. 10 (1937) trpt, fl, ob, cl, bn, 2 hn, vla, vc, pf (*ACA*)

CHOU WEN-CHUNG (b. 1923): Soliloquy of a Bhiksuni solo trpt, 4 hn, 3 trb, tba, 3 perc (*Pete*)

COBINE, ALBERT: Vermont Suite (1953) 4 trpt, 3 hn, 4 trb, bar, tba (*King*)

COOKE, A. (b. 1906): Sinfonietta trpt, WW 5tet, strg. 4tet, db (*Bel*)

COPLAND, AARON: Fanfare for the Common Man (1943) 3 trpt, 4 hn, 3 trb, tba, perc (*B & H*)

DEBUSSY, CLAUDE: Fanfares from *le Martyre de St. Sébastien* (1911) 4 trpts, 6 hn, 3 trb, tba, tym (*King*)

DELLO JOIO, NORMAN: To Saint Cecilia (1958) 3 trpts, 3 hn, 3 trb, tba, chor (*Fisc*)

DUKAS, PAUL: Fanfare pour précéder La Péri (1912) 3 trpts, 4 hn, 3 trb, tba (*Dur*)

GABRIELI, GIOVANNI: Canzona noni toni a 12 3 × 4 pt. br. choirs (*Pete*)

GIUFFRE, J. (b. 1921): Suspensions trpt, fl, al. sax, ten. sax, bn, hn, trb, vib, gtr, pf. perc (*MJQ*)

GOEHR, A. (b. 1932): The Deluge trpt, 2 voices, fl, hn, hp, strg. trio, db (*SchM*)

HINDEMITH, PAUL: Concert Music 3 trpts, 4 hn, 2 trb, tba, 2 hp, pf (*As*); Kammermusik No. 2 Op. 36 No. 1 solo pf, trpt, WW 5tet, b. cl, trb, strg. trio, db (*SchM*)

HOGG: Concerto 3 trpts, 3 hn, 3 trb, bar, tba (*King*)

IBERT, JACQUES: Capriccio (1939) trpt, strg. 4tet, fl, ob, cl, bn, hp (*Led*)

JESSON, ROY: Variations & Scherzo (1954) 4 trpts, 3 hn, 3 trb, bar, tba, tym, sn. dr. (*King*)

KAUFMANN, L. J.: Musik (1941) 3 trpts, 4 hn, 3 trb, tba (*HofL*)

KETTING, O.: Fanfares 8 trpts, 4 hn, 3 trb, tba, tym, perc (*Don*)

LANDRE, G. (b. 1905): Kammersymphonie trpt, WW 5tet, strg. 4tet, db, hp, perc (*Don*)

MADERNA, B. (b. 1920): Serenata trpt, fl, cl, b. cl, hn, hp, pf, vl, vla, db, perc (*SuvZ*)

MERILAINEN, USKO: Partita for Brass (1959) 4 trpts, 4 hn, 3 trb, tba (*King*)

MIHALOVICI, MARCEL: Etude en deux parties, Op. 64 (1952) 2 trpts, 2 cl, bn, trb, tba, cel, pf, perc (*Heu*)

MILHAUD, DARIUS: Création du Monde (1923) 2 trpts, 2 fl, ob, 2 cl, bn, hn, trb, al. sax, tym, perc, 2 vl, vc, pf (*Esc*); L'Homme et son Désir (1921) 2 trpts, picc, fl, ob, eng. hn, cl, b. cl, bn, hn, perc, hp, strg. 5tet (*UE*)

NAGEL, ROBERT: Divertimento for ten winds 2 trpts, fl, ob, cl, bn, 2 hn, trb, tba (*ACA*)

OTTERLOO, W. VAN (b. 1907): Intrada 4 trpts, 4 hn, bn, 4 trb, tba, tym, perc (*Don*)

PITTALUGA, GUSTAVO: Petite Suite (1935): trpt, fl, cl, bn, trb, hp, strg. 4tet (*Led*)

PLUISTER, S. (b. 1913): Divertimento trpt, 2 fl, ob, cl, hn, bn, tba, db, perc (*Don*)

POULENC, FRANCIS: Suite française (1935) 2 trpts, 3 trb, 2 ob, 2 bn, perc, pf (*Dur*)

PURCELL, HENRY: Symphony from *The Fairy Queen* 6 trpts, 2 hn, 3 trb, bar, tba (*King*)

RAUTAVAARA, EINO: A Requiem of Our Time (1958) 4 trpts, 4 hn, 3 trb, bar, tba, tym, perc (*King*)

READ, GARDNER: Sound Piece for Brass and Percussion (1950) 4 trpts, 4 hn, 3 trb, bar, 2 tba, tym, perc (*King*)

REYNOLDS, V.: Theme and Variations 3 trpts, 3 hn, 3 trb, bar, tba (*King*)

RIETI, VITTORIO (b. 1898): Madrigal trpt, WW 5tet, strg. 5tet, pf (*Sal*)

SCHULLER, GUNTHER (b. 1925): Symphony for Brass 6 trpts, 4 hn, 3 trb, bar, 2 tba, tym (*Sha*)

SCOTT, WAYNE: Rondo Giojoso (1956) 3 trpts, 4 hn, 4 trb, bar, tba, tym, perc (*King*)

STRAVINSKY, I.: Ragtime trpt, fl, cl, hn, trb, 2 vl, vla, db, cimbalom, perc (*Che*)

THOMSON, VIRGIL: Fanfare for France (1959) 3 trpts, 4 hn, 3 trb, perc (*B & H*)

TOMASI, H. (1901–71): Fanfare liturgique 3 trpts, 4 hn, 4 trb, tba, tym (*Led*)

VARÈSE, E.: Hyperprism 2 trpts, fl, cl, 3 hn, 2 trb, perc (*Cur*); Intégrales (1925) 2 trpts, 2 picc, 2 cl, ob, hn, 3 trb, 4 perc (*RicL*)

VAUGHAN WILLIAMS, R. (1872–1958): Scherzo alla marcia 2 trpts, 2 hn, 3 trb, fl, picc, 2 ob, 2 cl, 2 bn (*OUP*)

WOOLEN, RUSSELL: Triptych for Brass Choir Op. 34 (1957) 4 trpts, 2 hn, 3 trb, tba (*Pete*)

ZINDARS: The Brass Square 4 trpts, 4 hn, 3 trb, tba (*King*)

Key to Music Publishers shown in Works List
(U.K. agents given in brackets)·

ACA	American Composers' Alliance
And	Andraud
Andr	Andrieu Frères, Brussels, Belgium
Art	Artia, Prague, Czechoslovakia
As	Associated Music Publishers, 866 Third Ave., New York 10022 (G. Schirmer)
BA	Bärenreiter Ltd, 17–18 Bucklersbury, Hitchin, Herts SG5 1BB; Postfach 100329, D-3500 Kassel, Germany
Baro	M. Baron Company, Box 256, South Road, Oyster Bay, New York 11771
Bel	Belwin-Mills Music Ltd, 250 Purley Way, Croydon CR9 4QD, England; Melville, New York 11746
Benj	Anton J. Benjamin, Hamburg, Germany (Schauer)
BH-L	Breitkopf & Härtel, Karlstrasse 10, 701 Leipzig, Germany (Fentone)
B & H	Boosey & Hawkes Music Publishers Ltd, 295 Regent St., London W1R 8JH; Box 130, Oceanside, New York 11572
Bill	Editions Billaudot, 14 rue de l'Echiquier, Paris X, France (Kalmus)
Bom	Bomart, New York
Bote	Bote & Bock K.G., Hardenbergstrasse 9a, 1 Berlin 12, Germany
BroB	Broude Bros, 56 W. 45th St., New York, NY 10036 (Bärenreiter)
Brog	Editions Musicales Brogneaux, 73 ave Paul Janson, Brussels, Belgium
BrP	The Brass Press, 136 8th Avenue North, Nashville, Tenn. 37203 (EMERSON)

	Campbell Conelly & Co Ltd., 37 Soho Sq., London W1V 5DG
Cam	Camera Music Publishers, 23 LaFond Lane, Orinda, Calif. 94563 (G. Schirmer)
Can	Canzona Publications, P. O. Box 10123, Denver, Colo. 80210
Car	Carisch Edizioni Musicali, Via Gen. Fara 39, 20124 Milano, Italy (Peters/Boosey)
CBDM	CeBeDeM Foundation, 3 rue du Commerce, Brussels, Belgium (Lengnick)
Cham	Chamber Music Library, 168 Serpentine Road, Tenafly, New Jersey 07670
Che	J. & W. Chester Ltd, 7–9 Eagle Court, London EC1M 5QD, England (W. Hansen)
Cost	Editions Costallat, 60 rue de l'Echiquier, 75009 Paris, France (UMP)
Cur	J. Curwen & Sons Ltd, Kern House, 61–2 Lincoln's Inn Fields, WC2A 3XB (Faber/J. Schirmer)
Del	Georges Delrieu & Cie, Nice, France
Don	Donemus, 51 Jacob Obrechtstraat, Amsterdam, Holland (Kalmus)
Dur	Editions Durand & Cie, 4 Place de la Madeleine, Paris, France (UMP)
EdMa	Edition Marbot, Hamburg, W. Germany
EdMb	Editio Musica Budapest, Hungary (Boosey)
EdMT	Editions Musicales Transatlantiques, 14 Ave Hoche, 75008 Paris, France
ElkH	Henri Elkan Music Publisher, 1316 Walnut Street, Philadelphia, Pa 19107 (UMP)
Eme	Emerson Edition, Windmill Farm, Ampleforth, Yorks
Ens	Ensemble Publications, Box 98, Buffalo, NY 14222
Esc	Editions Max Eschig, 48 rue de Rome, 75008 Paris, France (Schott)
Eul	Edition Eulenburg, Zurich, Switzerland (Schott)
Euro	European American Music Corp., 195 Allwood Rd., Clifton, N.J. 07012 (Kalmus)
E-V	Elkan-Vogal Co. Inc. (UMP)
Fab	Faber Music Ltd, 3 Queen Square, London WC1N 3AU
Fel	Felseckers Erben, Nurnberg, Germany
Fen	Fentone Music Ltd, 20 Earlham St., London WC2H 9LN
Fisc	Carl Fischer Inc., 62 Cooper Sq., New York 10003 (Boosey)
Gen	General Music Publishing Co., 116 Boylston St., Boston, Mass. 02116

Gerv	Gervan Edition Musicale, 352 Ave de la Couronne, Brussels, Belgium
Gras	Editions Gras, 36 rue Pope Charpentier, La Flèche, France
Gray	H. W. Gray & Co. (Belwin)
HanW	Wilhelm Hansen Musikforlag, Gothersgade 9–11, 1123 Copenhagen K, Denmark
Has	Carl Haslinger, Tuchlauben 11. Vienna 1, Austria
Hein	Heinrichshofen Verlag, Wilhelmshaven, Germany (Peters)
Hel	Helicon Press, The Old Malthouse, Knight St., Sawbridgeworth, Herts
Henn	Editions Henn, 8 rue de Hesse, 1211 Geneva, Switzerland (UMP)
Heu	Heugel et Cie, 2 bis, rue Vivienne, Paris, France (UMP)
Hinn	Hinnenthal, Bielefeld, Germany
HofL	Veb Friedrich Hofmeister, Karlstrasse 10, 701 Leipzig, E. Germany (Fentone)
IIM	Istituto Interamericano Musicologia
Int	International Music Co., 545 Fifth Avenue, New York 10017 (Kalmus)
Is	Israeli Music Publications, Box 6011, Tel Aviv, Israel (Peters)
KalA	A. A. Kalmus Ltd, 38 Eldon Way, Paddock Wood, Tonbridge, Kent
King	Robert King Music Co., 112A Main Street, North Easton, Mass. 02356 (Emerson/Belwin)
Kis	F. Kistner & C. F. Siegel, Cologne, Germany (Novello)
L-AM	Latin-American Music Publishing Co. (Southern)
Led	Alphonse Leduc Editions Musicales, 175 rue Saint Honoré, 75001 Paris, France (UMP)
Leed	Leeds Music Ltd (MCA Music Ltd)
Lem	Henri Lemoine et Cie, 17 rue Pigalle, Paris, France (UMP)
Len	Alfred Lengnick & Co. Ltd., 421a Brighton Road, South Croydon CR2, Surrey
Leu	Verlag F. E. C. Leuckart, Munich, Germany (Novello)
Lie	Musikverlag Robert Lienau, Berlin-Lichterfelde, Germany (Peters)
Mark	E. B. Marks Music Ltd (Belwin)
Math	Mathot Editions, Paris (Salabert)
M & M	McGinnis & Marx, 133 Seventh Avenue, New York, 10014
MCA	MCA Music Ltd, 138 Piccadilly, London W1V 9FN

Men	Mentor Music, 17 Broadview Drive, Brookfield, Conn. 06804
Merc	Mercury Music Co. Ltd, (Novello)
MJQ	MJQ Music Inc., 17 West 60th St., New York, 10023
Mosc	Moscow State Publishing House, USSR
MS	MS Publications, 1045 Garfield, Oak Park, Illinois 60304
Mue	Willy Mueller, Heidelberg, Germany (Novello)
MusR	Musica Rara, Le Traversier, Chemin de la Buire, 84170 Monteux, France
NewM	New Music Edition (Pressler)
Noe	Otto Heinrich Noetzel Verlag, Wilhelmshaven, Germany
Nors	Norsk Musikforlag A. S., Box 1499, Vika, Oslo 1, Norway (Chester)
Nov	Novello & Co. Ltd, 8 Lower James St., London W1R 4DN
OUP	Oxford University Press, Walton Street, Oxford OX2 6DP; 200 Madison Ave., New York 10016
P-AU	Pan-American Union
Peer	Peer International Library Ltd (Southern)
Pete	Peters Edition Ltd, 119–25 Wardour St., London W1V 4DN; 373 Park Ave. South, New York 10016
Ph	Philharmusica Corp., 110 W. Crooked Hill Rd., Pearl River, NY 10965
Pizz	Pizzi
Pr	Theodore Presser Co., Presser Place, Bryn Mawr, Pa. 19010 (Kalmus)
	Pressler Edition, PO Box 521, D-8000 Munich 1, W. Germany
Rem	Remick
RicL	G. Ricordi & Co (London) Ltd, The Bury, Church St., Chesham, Bucks
Rong	Rongwen
Rou	Rouart, Lerolle & Cie (Salabert)
Sal	Editions Salabert, 575 Madison Ave., New York 10022 (UMP)
	Schauer & May Ltd, 67 Belsize Lane, London NW3 5AX
Sche	Scherzando Editions Musicales, 14 rue Auguste Orts, Brussels, Belgium
SchG	G. Schirmer Ltd, Kern House, 61–2 Lincoln's Inn Fields, London WC2A 3XB; 866 Third Ave., New York 10022
SchL	Schott & Co. Ltd, 48 Gt Marlborough St., London W1V 2BN
SchM	B. Schott's Soehne, Mainz, W. Germany
Schmi	C. F. Schmidt, Heilbronn a.N., Germany

Schw	Edition Schwann, Frankfurt, W. Germany (Peters)
See	Seesaw Music Corp., 2067 Broadway, New York 10023 (Southern)
Sha	Shawnee Press, Delaware Water Gap, Pa 18327 (Kalmus)
Siko	Musikverlag Hans Sikorski, Hamburg, Germany (Belwin/ Campbell)
SM	Süddeutscher Musikverlag
So	Southern Music Publishing Co. Ltd, 8 Denmark St., London WC2H 8LT
SoNY	Southern Music Publishing Co., 1740 Broadway, New York 10019
SouT	Southern Music Co., Box 329, San Antonio, Texas 78292 (Belwin)
	Stainer & Bell Ltd, 82 High Road, London N2 9PW
SuvZ	Edizioni Suvini Zerboni SpA, Galleria del Corso 4, Milano, Italy
Tem	Tempo Music Publications, 21 Frederick St., London WC1X 0ND; Box 392, Chicago, Illinois 60690
Tri	Tritone Press
Tro	Tromba Publications, 1859 York St., Denver, Colo. 80206
UMP	United Music Publishers Ltd, 42 Rivington St., London EC2A 3BN
UE	Universal Edition (London) Ltd, 2–3 Fareham St., London W1V 4DV
Univ	University Music Press, Box 1267, Ann Arbor, Mich. 48106
War	Warner Bros Music Ltd, 17 Berners St., London W1P 3DD; 265 Secaucus Rd, Secaucus, NJ 07094
Wein	Weintraub Music Co., 33 West 60th St., New York 10023
Will	Joseph Williams Ltd (Stainer & Bell)
WIM	Western International Music, 2859 Holt Ave., Los Angeles, Calif. 90034
Wimb	Wimbledon Music Inc., 1888 Century Park East, Century City, Calif. 90067 (G. Schirmer)
Wit	Witmark
Zim	Wilhelm Zimmermann, Frankfurt-am-Main, Germany (Novello)